Nikki Sixx is an international rock icc
and Sixx:A.M., three-time *New York*
Heroin Diaries, This Is Gonna Hurt, a
thropist, photographer, and addiction
ber one nationally syndicated rock ra
on iHeart Media, for eight years. In
Crüe's hit Netflix biopic, The Dirt, ba_

C000264444

Praise for *The First 21*

'A deeply personal plunge into Sixx's dysfunctional upbringing . . . The journey
from Feranna to Sixx – a name he maybe, sort of stole from another local musician
who had dubbed himself Niki Syxx – is a fraught and complicated one. But it's a
story that Sixx shares with humor and honesty' *USA Today*

'Amazing . . . *The First 21: How I Became Nikki Sixx* is the origin story many have
been waiting for . . . There are many poignant moments and stunning revelations.
You'll learn how he went from sweeping floors to selling out shows at The Starwood, the artists and authors who inspired him, the meaning behind the trade-
mark black lines he wears onstage, how he ripped off everything from Johnny
Thunders' look to the name Nikki Sixx, and how James Caan almost lassoed him
poolside. However, his determination to succeed is the real story' *Aquarian*

'[Nikki] writes it in a way where the reader feels like they're there' Dr. Phil

'[*The First 21*] explores how [Nikki Sixx's] hand-to-mouth upbringing made him
hungry to see his rock-band dreams come to fruition . . . thoughtful glimpses into
the backstory of a very determined musician' *Kirkus Reviews*

'[Nikki Sixx] follows his searing memoir, *The Heroin Diaries*, with an equally
exhilarating look at the first 21 years of his life . . . Fans will relish this passionate
look at the man behind the hair' *Publishers Weekly*

'A fascinating read, one that Sixx tells with candor and an awareness of self that
few possess' *Audio Ink Radio*

'This is a profound true story finding identity, of how Frank Feranna became Nikki
Sixx. It's also a road map to the ways you can overcome anything, and achieve all
of your goals, if only you put your mind to it' *BraveWords*

Also by Nikki Sixx

The Dirt:
Confessions of the World's Most Notorious Rock Band
with Tommy Lee, Mick Mars, Vince Neil, and Neil Strauss

The Heroin Diaries:
A Year in the Life of a Shattered Rock Star

This Is Gonna Hurt:
Music, Photography, and
Life Through the Distorted Lens of Nikki Sixx

THE FIRST 21

HOW I BECAME NIKKI SIXX

by

Frank Feranna

and

Nikki Sixx

CONSTABLE

CONSTABLE

First published in the USA in 2021 by Hachette Books, an imprint of
Perseus Books, LLC, a subsidiary of Hachette Book Group, Inc.
This edition published in Great Britain in 2021 by Constable
This paperback edition published in 2022 by Constable.

1 3 5 7 9 10 8 6 4 2

A CIP catalogue record for this book is available from the British Library.

ISBN: 978-1-40871-613-7

Cover design by Richard Ljoenes

Cover photographs: Nikki in 1989 © Koh Hasebe/Shinko Music/Getty Images; the Sunset
Strip at night © Scott Robinson/*Los Angeles Times*; concert flyer from the collection of Max and
Sherri Mazursky; Frank Feranna at seventeen or eighteen and Frank on Christmas Eve 1978
© Angie Diehl; vinyl record © Shutterstock; all other images courtesy of the author.

Cover copyright © 2021 Hachette Book Group, Inc.

Endpaper design copyright © Joe Lalich; endpaper art copyright © United States Geological Survey

Photographs courtesy of the author with the following exceptions: In the first scrapbook, photograph
of Susie Maddox and Frankie, courtesy of Susan Bond; photograph of Ramon and family with Deanna,
courtesy of Ramon Rodriguez; Seattle photographs, courtesy of Richard Van Zandt. On page 75,
photograph of Don, Sharon, and Michele, courtesy of Michele Amburgey. In the second scrapbook,
cover photograph courtesy of Katie Kastel; photograph of Frank Feranna, library card, and work ID,
courtesy of Angie Diehl; photographs on the third scrapbook page, courtesy of Angie Diehl and Don
Adkins; and photographs of London and the Starwood, courtesy of Don Adkins. Photographs on pages
147, 167, and 176, courtesy of Don Adkins. Photograph on page 202, courtesy of Ryan Dorgan. Map
elements courtesy of the US Geological Survey. Elements of design throughout by Joe Lalich.

Printed and bound in Great Britain by Clays Ltd, Elcograf, S.p.A.

Papers used by Constable are from well-managed forests and other responsible sources.

Constable
An imprint of
Little, Brown Book Group
Carmelite House
50 Victoria Embankment
London EC4Y 0DZ

An Hachette UK Company

www.hachette.co.uk
www.littlebrown.co.uk

This book is for my family,
so that you may better understand
my heart, my dedication, my lust for life,
and my love for you.

Contents

1. The Stadium Tour   1

2. Snake River   17

3. Just Kids   27

4. Nona and Tom   37

5. Twin Falls   55

6. Jerome   71

7. McCleary's Drugstore   83

8. Seattle   95

9. Teenage Wasteland   101

10. Diamond Dogs   107

11. Back on the Farm   115

12. Los Angeles   119

13. Eruption   127

14. London Calling   135

15. The Spotlight   143

16. Nikki Nine   151

17. Niki Syxx   159

18. Nigel   161

19. The Starwood   169

20. New Monster   181

21. Stick to Your Guns   195

Acknowledgments   203

THE FIRST 21

The Stadium Tour

Chapter 1

Spring in Los Angeles, seventy-something degrees, and my agent, Dennis Arfa, had taken me out to the ball game. The Dodgers were up in the seventh. Dennis was working on his second hot dog with not a care in the world. So naturally, in the snarkiest voice I could muster, I asked him, "Why didn't *we* ever play Dodger Stadium?"

I've been working with Dennis for many a year, and he knows the places we've played as well as we do: Budokan, Wembley, Red Rocks, Madison Square Garden. Mötley Crüe's opened for the Rolling Stones. We've packed every outdoor shed we've been booked into and headlined outdoor festivals around the world. In Los Angeles, we've filled the Hollywood Bowl and sold out the Staples Center. But Dodger Stadium? The only time I'd set foot on the field was to throw out a ceremonial first pitch.

"I guess the reason would have to be your bright idea to break up the band."

Both of us burst out laughing.

"If you guys ever change your minds," Dennis said, "just call me."

A few hours later, I woke my wife up.

"If we ever get back together, we're going to play Dodger Stadium."

Courtney's used to me waking her up after midnight. Most of the time, she'll indulge me. This time she said, "But, baby, the band signed a contract."

This was true. A few years earlier, Mötley Crüe signed a "secession of touring" contract—and Courtney knows that I am a man of my word. But I'm also a man who's ruled by his passions.

"I'll think of something," I said.

At the time, I was working on *The Dirt*—a movie based on the book about Mötley. The book had been a major best seller, and so far the movie was turning out better than any of us would have guessed. Tommy was being portrayed by Machine Gun Kelly. An English actor named Douglas Booth was playing me. So Booth was doing his best Nikki Sixx while the real Nikki Sixx was taking meetings with Live Nation, Apple, Spotify, radio stations, and social media platforms to promote the film. I'd show scenes and snippets from the movie, share some of my own memories, and play the new song I'd written.

Actually, I had several new songs—well-formed ideas that all seemed exciting. I had been woodshedding with John 5, a guitarist who's played with everyone from k.d. lang to Marilyn Manson and Rob Zombie, and with Sahaj Ticotin, a musician who'd set a record for holding a note longer than any other male singer. We had made a bunch of demos, and I played them all for Bob Rock, who'd helped make Mötley Crüe's biggest album, *Dr. Feelgood*, in 1989. Hard to believe thirty years had gone by. But when Bob heard the tracks, he said, "These sound like classic Mötley Crüe songs." The song I had written for the credit sequence reminded Bob of "Kickstart My Heart"—high praise from the man who'd produced the original.

"We have the songs," I told Courtney.

The songs—the music—is where it all starts. Without the music, there'd be no club tours. No theater tours. No arenas. No private jets getting us to the arenas. There'd be no money, no platinum records to hang on the studio walls. For Mötley, there would have been none of the love and the hate or the death and destruction that come with the lifestyle. Between the four of us, we've got 160 years' worth of memories to draw on. If this were a VH1 special, we'd all say in unison, "Some of the best we've had! Some of the worst! And not many that we would take back!"

We'd all be telling the truth. As a kid, I drew bands in my notebooks. Four complementary characters with superhero-like powers on drums, bass, guitar, and vocals. Those guys always looked cool and always had the best songs, played them well, and the lyrics had something to say. In my mind, I was building a new kind of monster.

Those bands were Mötley in embryo form. All I had to do was move out to Los Angeles, learn to play bass, and find three other musicians who saw the world the way I did. In the end, that's what happened. Of course, it took a ton of hard work, and not just the work you'd imagine. On top of writing, rehearsing, working on our look and stage show, and playing—and playing, and playing—there were the constant demands, obligations the industry made: junkets. Interviews with journalists who drank our booze, did our drugs, and then turned around and slagged us in their magazines. It took years of band therapy to keep us together and remind us of all the reasons we had to keep going.

But I had my own family to look after too. At the time, Courtney was pregnant. Our daughter, Ruby, was due in July. Touring isn't the easiest thing to do when you've got small kids at home. Over the years, I missed more holidays than I could count. I missed birthdays. There were PTA meetings I wanted to go to, but you can't hop a flight from Japan when the rest of the band's on their way to Australia.

I couldn't blame Courtney if she didn't want me to go. If she asked me to stay, I'd stay. If she *didn't* ask me to stay, my feelings would be hurt. But now that I'd brought it up, we both knew I wouldn't stop thinking about it.

"You have the songs," Courtney admitted before drifting back off to her sweet, mysterious dreams.

"Live Wire." "Looks that Kill." "Shout at the Devil." It's the hit songs that made us a hit band. They're what the audience craves and demands. The audience is a big part of the monster we've built, and much as we love to play deep cuts and covers and songs we've just written, we give the monster the red meat it needs.

The new stuff is important. Without it, we'd be stuck in stasis and turn into a cover band: Mötley Crüe plays Mötley Crüe.

But it's just as important to keep writing hits. We can still smell one when it comes along. We're the same band we were on day one. The same four guys. Older and smarter and no longer starving, but lean and efficient and fifteen thousand days wiser than we used to be. Sometimes we've been smart enough to keep going. Sometimes we've known when to quit.

Early on, we learned a lesson. Up in Grass Valley, Nevada, we'd gone on a radio show. It was the first time we'd been on a radio station. But when we did an in-store, later that day, no one came. We stood there, looking through records, pretending to shop. Three guys with blue-black hair, one guy with bleached hair, and we just happened to be buying records! A few hours earlier, we'd been so excited. Now, nobody knew who we were. We didn't want to be seen like that, standing around, shuffling our feet, looking disheartened. As we were leaving, we saw a cool-looking guy with long hair.

I was like, "Oh, there's another musician!"

"Hey, how you doing?" I said.

"Hey, what's going on?"

"You're in a band? I am too!"

The guy nodded.

I asked him, "What band?"

"Supertramp."

I was a Supertramp fan. There were some Supertramp songs I loved. But before I could ask any questions, the guy said the one thing you usually don't want to hear from an old band you've loved: "We just recorded two new ones."

"Oh! That's amazing." I wasn't cynical about it.

"Yeah," he said. "We never talk. People live in all different places. One guy in England, one in Florida. I live here, so we recorded the twenty-four-track parts and shipped them to each other."

"You didn't play them together?"

"We never even saw each other. I didn't talk to them once."

The guys and I walked back to the van in a daze.

"You have to promise that will never happen to us."

"No way, dude. We're brothers for life."

But lo and behold, when we recorded new tracks for our own greatest hits, we weren't on speaking terms either. We weren't speaking when we wrote *The Dirt*. Each of us worked on our chapters in private. We didn't even look at each other's parts until the whole thing was assembled.

That wouldn't have worked out so well on the stage.

For us, it had become impossible to paper over the cracks that start showing after five years or ten—and by that point, we had been going for twenty.

When you're young, you can show up hungover, wearing the clothes you've been wearing all week, and somehow you look good. You look good in your tight pants and heels and have all your hair. Then one day you wake up, and it all takes more effort. Musically, you may have gotten much better, but physically, it's become more of a drain. Getting out on the road is a drain. Staying out on the road is a drain. Onstage, you feel the same, but it takes longer each time to recover, and dealing with the other guys can be exasperating.

For every rock band that's able to push past that point, there must be thousands that fail. Maybe we didn't because we were balanced just right in a few crucial ways. But there were certainly times when I wouldn't have bet on our long-term survival.

Tommy is extremely driven. That's an invaluable thing when we see eye to eye.

Mick doesn't care about anything except for his parts and his tone. He doesn't care about pyro, costumes, the stage show, or anything else—he only cares about his guitar. He plays so loud, we've all got hearing damage. But that's who Mick was when we met him, and it's who Mick is today.

Vince is a Gatling gun. He blows in. He does his thing, and it's usually two hundred proof. Then he goes off on his own, like a wolf or a lone samurai.

Often enough, that adds up to a functional unit. When we're in agreement, we're driven, passionate, and very focused: "*This* is who we are. This is who we were born to be. This is what people want from us, and this is how we deliver the mail." But when Tommy and I aren't seeing eye to eye, Mick's being passive, Vince can't be bothered, and I have a bee in my bonnet that's driving all of us crazy, it takes more than flowers and candy to get us in line.

Historically, one of the problems we've had is our communication. Early on, I would insist on rehearsing whole sets, playing backward from the encore, then forward again, building our intros, breaking every song down, remaking it, breaking it back down one more time. It was relentless. To the other guys, it might have seemed frivolous and redundant, and we did it seven days a week. The only way *out* of this vicious circle of rehearsal was to have a gig, but the only way to do a gig was to have new music or a new song. Then, when we did have new songs, it meant booking a gig at the Whisky, the Starwood, the Troubadour, or doing dates up the West Coast. The band had to be working and focused, and my focus was always full-time on the band. I was obsessed. Being obsessed was the only way to get great, to get ready, to know in our bones that we could compete with the big boys. But it didn't make me the easiest person to get along with. I'm not always a walk in the park, and as we've gotten older, some of the other guys are like, "Dude, don't tell me what to do."

That's a good thing. When we were younger, they'd just seethe and snipe behind my back, and I ignored it for ten years or twenty, until it all came up in band therapy.

Most of the time, we get past it. Sometimes I'll storm off. But then I'll remember what life was like before Mötley.

Going down to the Starwood on punk night, alone. I'd be in heels, a band like Fear would be playing, and someone would scream in my face, "You're a faggot!" Or I'd get spit on and I'd throw my glass—not the drink out of my glass, but the actual glass. I'd bust the guy's forehead open. Then I'd get my ass kicked and get thrown out of the club.

The other guys in the band were the same way. Lock us in a room, and we'd fight like crazy. Vince and Tommy would get into it, I'd get in the middle to break them up, and we'd all end up with black eyes—except for Mick, who just watched and shook his head. But out in the world, we were different, a united front. One time, after a long night of drinking, a guy with a Fu Manchu moustache offered us all amyl nitrite. I was too far gone to try it, but Tommy and Vince did, and right away they started fighting. I went to break them up, and we were scuffling when four or five dudes walked over to us: "Hey, what the fuck are you doing?"

We turned and jumped those guys. After we'd beaten the shit out of them, Tommy and Vince went back to fighting each other. When they were punched out, we went into the parking lot and shared a bottle of Jack.

That was Mötley Crüe *on* speaking terms.

Not the most functional band in the world. But functional enough when it mattered. By the time *The Dirt* film came around, we had gotten back to a good place. Seventy-three million people watched the film. In the studio, with Bob Rock back in the producer's seat, we had recorded those new songs—and they really had sounded like real Mötley Crüe songs.

I'd driven around LA, listening to them on repeat, looking for flaws.

After a week of that, I had decided, "These songs hold up."

After that, I'd called Tommy.

"Roll your eyes," I had said. "But doesn't it just feel like something is missing?"

"Like what?"

"Like touring."

"But didn't we promise that we wouldn't tour?"

"I know. I know."

It took a while to convince him that sometimes a promise is meant to be broken. There *was* a way out of the contract we signed—but only if all four of us agreed to it. If all of us weren't on board, none of us could be.

"Nikki, we told everyone we're done with touring," Vince had said.

"I know. I know."

We got Vince to agree to a meeting. Mick was curious too. We talked to our manager, partner, and label head, Allen Kovac, who had already made a few calls of his own.

Allen Kovac is a genius. He's the guy who helped us get our masters back from Elektra—and, in doing so, made a real difference industry-wide. He's been with us for twenty-seven years. He's my personal manager as well as the band's. And for all those years, we've only ever operated on a handshake.

I would trust him with my life. I might even trust him with my wife.

"If you're serious," Allen had told us, "Live Nation's interested in a big way."

Now it was time to speak to Dennis again.

"The movie's exciting," I'd told him. "But if we did tour, would it have the same charge that it used to? We've done a million arena tours. If we were to do this, what would be different?"

"Live Nation doesn't want an arena tour. They want to do stadiums."

"Does that mean Dodger Stadium?"

Dennis laughed. "Yes," he had said. "Aren't you glad we went to that baseball game?"

In 2019, only a few guitar bands could pack a stadium, much less go out on a stadium tour. U2. Radiohead. Springsteen and the E Street Band, in their prime, could have probably sold out the state of New Jersey, but would they have racked up the same numbers all over the place that Taylor Swift or Beyoncé could have drawn? I'm not so sure. The clubs we'd started out playing held a few hundred people. Theaters could hold a few thousand, and arenas fit thousands more. (Madison Square Garden's a good place to play, and it holds about twenty.) Next came the outdoor sheds: anywhere from fifteen to thirty thousand. But stadiums, which start at around thirty thousand and can be triple that size, have always been the holy grail.

It was ambitious. But every time I hear "rock is dead" or "guitar bands are dead," all it does is light a fire. Technology has its place, but I don't like rock and roll that's made on laptops. I don't like the idea of dragging and dropping loops, moving this hook or chopping that part up and putting it somewhere else. The older I get, the more I want single takes of a performance. I want to leave the mistakes in, move on, and be raw. I tell Courtney all the time, "I want to do a record like *Led Zeppelin I* or the first Aerosmith album. Write the songs, go to some shitty rehearsal room, eat shitty pizza, cut the album, mix it, and release it." I'm not a person who likes to go slow—I don't believe anything sounds better than real guitars, real drums, and real bass playing real songs with a history that goes from Chuck Berry and Little Richard to Aerosmith and AC/DC. And I've played for millions of people, so I know that millions believe the same thing.

All in all, it took a couple of band meetings—but a $100 million offer can be very convincing.

The guys in Def Leppard are all friends of ours. They stepped up to say, "No question. We want to do this with you." After that, we didn't think of the bands we wanted to go out with as supporting acts. Plenty of people were crunching the numbers. We were more focused on throwing a party. An around-the-world celebration for us and the fans.

Early on, we asked David Lee Roth.

"I don't open for bands that I influenced," he said.

I shook my head. "Dude. You're gonna play in front of eighty thousand people! When is the last time David Lee Roth played for eighty thousand people?"

We were all big fans of David's. We've always been fans of Van Halen. Obviously, we'd been influenced by them—who hadn't? But David passed.

Joan Jett was next on our list. We ranked Joan highly not only because of her songs, which we loved, but also because she's always been a real pleasure to work and hang out with. Thankfully, she didn't play hard to get. Now it was us, Joan Jett, and Def Leppard. Then the boys and girls in market research told us we needed to get one more band from that era.

Poison was the band they settled on.

We were not thrilled. The four of us felt that Mötley had been there from the get-go. Metallica, Mötley Crüe, and U2—for us, those were the bands from the era that came to mind. Guns N' Roses came later, and that was a hard band to argue with too. But then there had been an onslaught of bands we didn't feel were really real. Bands fabricated by industry people who'd said, "We need our own Mötley Crüe. We need a blond singer and three guys like that." The same thing happened with alternative bands later on: you had Nirvana and Pearl Jam, and then you had a lot of bands that looked and sounded a bit like Nirvana and Pearl Jam but were just watered-down, lightweight versions of the original.

Well, it turned out we were wrong. Our fans wanted what they wanted, and what they wanted was us and Def Leppard, Joan Jett, and Poison—and if we were going to go out and tour one more time, we were going to give our fans just what they wanted: hours and hours of hit songs delivered with musicianship, attitude, and the biggest show they've ever seen.

With that lineup in place, we put eight shows on sale. They sold out right away. Eight more shows sold out just as quickly. Eight *more* shows—same story.

We all thought, "Wow, what a nice way to celebrate the movie! What a great way to go out one last time!"

With twenty-four shows booked and counting, I knew I'd have to shift, full-time, to training mode.

———

Every musician has his or her own way of going about it. For me, training mode is a beast with multiple tentacles. There's the physical part, the mental part, the emotional part, and the musical part. Stage design comes next, along with broad concepts and an overview of what the whole show is going to look like, what it represents, what we've all got to say, and why right now is the right time to say it. But physical conditioning makes everything else possible, and for Mötley, that's deeply entwined with our setlist.

We build each one out of five-minute segments. Technically, some of our songs are shorter or a little longer, which also leaves time in between songs if one of us wants to talk to the audience. In reality, you can only use up so much time. Before you know it, you break curfew, the promoter gets fined, and the band's looking at fines: suddenly we're paying $50,000 for going one song over the limit. In some places—Europe, Japan—if the band goes too late, people can't take the subway or train back home, plus the promoters will actually turn off the power. If you truly care about people, you can't just go out there and jam. So at five minutes a song, we build out, in accordance with the kind of show we'll be playing: two hours if it's just us. Ninety minutes if we're the headliner. Those lengths dictate our workouts too.

What I've done, going all the way back to the days of cassette tapes, is print the setlist out and put it right next to wherever I'm going to do cardio. If we're opening with "Kickstart My Heart," I'm going to burst through the door with guns blazing. If the third song's going to be "Home Sweet Home," I know that I can slow down to a walk on the treadmill. If the next song is "Wild Side," I'll kick it back up—but "Wild Side" has a breakdown halfway through it, and I know I'll be able to catch my breath then. With a lot of bands, you'll look over at the guitarist halfway through the set and see that he's panting. I factor the stamina it takes to avoid that into my workouts, timing each segment to match all the songs.

That's ninety minutes flat-out on the treadmill, followed by two hours of weights. After that, I'll spend another hour and a half with my bass, sitting and playing the songs straight through in order. Eventually, I've built my stamina up to the point where I'm doing the entire show physically and musically without feeling destroyed. Then I'll do the whole musical part standing up. That's one more thing that can trip a band up. You sit down and play and think you're in pretty good shape. But get out on stage, and the same thing will kill you.

I carry the setlist with me long after it's been memorized. I tape it next to the bathroom mirror and to the side of the fridge—that way, I have to see it whenever I want some ice cream. For the stadium tour, we hired trainers and a nutritionist. All of a sudden, we were all watching our intake of proteins, carbs, and greens and keeping track of the calories we burned. The nutritionist made sure we ate enough to get through our workouts while maintaining a five-hundred-calorie-a-day deficit.

It might not sound very sexy, but if you want to compete—if you want to *stay* in the ring with the big boys—you find yourself doing whatever it takes.

Before long, I was shredded. My stamina was way up. Mentally and emotionally, I was fully charged, fired up, feeling inspired whenever I picked up a bass or guitar. And because my health is directly connected to my creativity, I could barely go out to the store to buy milk without getting ten new ideas I'd have to pull over to write down.

On the Final Tour, we had twenty-one trucks and buses carrying us and the gear. We'd built a roller coaster for Tommy and his rotating drum kit. We'd put on the biggest pyro show anyone had put on, anywhere, ever. We lit the whole top of our lighting rig and had flames shooting *down* at us while we played. The whole band was covered in fire retardant—a clear spray applied to our stage clothes. We had fire extinguishers set up at twenty-foot intervals and buckets full of rags soaking in water in case any of us caught fire. On past tours, Tommy had gotten burned. I've been burned more times than I can remember. Your mom told you this, and I'm telling you now: if you're playing with fire, you're going to get burned. But we've always loved playing with fire. When Mötley Crüe started out, it was simple: I'd cover myself in lighter fluid, and Vince would ignite me—no tricks. Down and dirty. Something a little more advanced, going all the way back to 1981, would have been snaking a wire down from a nine-volt battery to a little cage in the heels of my boots. That ignited pyro chips—my boots would be smoking—and in a small club, it looked cool: "What the fuck? The guy's boots are on fire!"

But in a much bigger space, you wouldn't have even seen it.

For the Final Tour, we put a flamethrower on my bass. It weighed one hundred pounds and shot thirty-foot flames. I could also ignite my mic stand, which we had suspended on chains. Those chains allowed me to grab the mic stand and throw it. A burning mic stand flying through the air is something you can see clear to the back rows and still think, "That looks awesome."

We had acrobats. We had fireworks. We had one crane for me and another for Vince. We should have called it the Holy Fuck Tour—and the stadium tour's set design had to top it. Because we'd taken pyro about as far as pyro could go, I wanted to see if we could top ourselves while using no pyro at all.

Our production manager, Robert Long, has been with us for a very long time because he makes the impossible happen. I don't like to hear, "It can't be done." For me, "can't be done" is just a starting point. "No one's ever done that before"—that's not a challenge for us, it's a given, and that's where technology comes into play. For this tour, we wanted big screens. Super-powerful imagery.

"We're picturing a postapocalyptic, Japanese-type environment with giant robots," I said to Robert.

"Okay," he said, getting excited. "We've got projectors now that can roll up and disappear. We'll set up meetings with the laser companies—I know you guys have talked about using lasers instead of fire, but I see a way of doing both. If you want to reconsider 'no pyro,' we've got pyro now that can shoot jets of flame into balls of flame. You won't believe the effects we can do."

I'm open to new ideas—as long as they top all our old ones. I'm always trying to outdo myself. I'm always trying to outdo Tommy, and Tommy's the same way with me: "I want to go upside down. I want to fly over the crowd. I want to do something no one's even thought of!" Tommy can hit just as hard upside down, and while Tommy and I are pushing each other, Mick's working on getting his guitar to sound bigger and louder than anything we've heard before. I don't have to compete with Mick on technique. I like to play simpler—a little more punk rock, a little more in the pocket, like Cliff Williams from AC/DC. I have some big riffs, but mostly I like to stay where I feel sexy and dirty. That's it: four people creating a sound that's blown past every obstacle anyone's put in our way. Seeing us do that onstage every night makes the fans realize they can do the same thing with whatever challenges they might be facing. I know, because when the lights come on at the end of the night, I see the change in their faces. We all see it, and we carry that with us to the next town. That's what rock and roll *is* at the most basic level. It's what fuels Mötley Crüe—and we try not to take it for granted, even though it takes a lot out of you too.

We knew that because of our families, our ages—because of the years we spent pushing our luck physically, chemically, karmically—we didn't have many years left as a band. What we did have was one hell of a consolation prize: twenty-nine stadium shows packed into three months that were going to go by like a bullet. And that was only the start of the tour. Behind the scenes, we were led to believe there were a hundred more shows in the offing.

It was a good thing we'd gotten in shape.

We decided to call it the Stadium Tour. Starting in Texas, at the Alamodome, we were playing all over the country before ending up back in Los Angeles, where we were scheduled to play a Labor Day show at SoFi Stadium. Not Dodger Stadium, like Dennis had promised. But there was a consolation prize for that as well: SoFi Stadium is much bigger.

Live Nation announced the dates in December, leaving me seven months to spend at home. Planning ahead, I scheduled breaks in between shows to maximize time with Courtney and the kids. It hasn't always been easy, balancing my family's needs and the band's. This time, it felt like I'd gotten the formula right. I kept up with my workouts. I ironed out the details so that, out on the road, we could stay focused on what we'd be doing onstage. I crossed all the *t*'s I could see, spent my days dotting the *i*'s. The weeks flew by, and it wasn't until February that I was out driving and heard a report on the news: A virus was spreading. The start of a pandemic, the newscaster said.

By the end of the month, a football stadium with eighty thousand screaming fans was the last place anyone in the world would have wanted to be.

Snake River

Chapter 2

The Continental Divide runs through northwest Wyoming, and just below Yellowstone National Park there's a body of water called Two Ocean Creek. Where the creeks split, the streams run in opposite directions, toward the two oceans that give them their names.

Atlantic Creek flows into the Yellowstone, Missouri, and Mississippi Rivers before emptying into the Gulf of Mexico, more than three thousand miles from its source.

Pacific Creek flows into Snake River, which runs through Idaho toward Oregon before turning upward along the state border and then turning westward again, toward Washington and the Pacific Ocean.

A trail takes you out to the point where the two streams diverge. You can reach down, put your hands in the cold, swirling water. Turn them one way, and those waters will flow into one of the oceans. Turn them a little bit more, and the waters will end up three time zones away.

This was the part of the country we moved to when COVID-19 knocked the world off its axis. Courtney and I had been talking for years about finding a new home for ourselves. We looked in Nashville, but Nashville was too far away. We looked in Vegas, but that was before we knew we were pregnant—Vegas was not the place to raise our baby girl. After the Stadium Tour, we were going to look one more time. Then the tour was postponed, Los Angeles went into lockdown, and COVID-19 made it look less and less like the place where we wanted to be.

One morning, Courtney whispered to me, "I want you to have an open mind."

Usually I'll dig my heels in before even listening to what comes next. This time all Courtney had to say was, "Wyoming."

I knew immediately that she was right.

Wyoming has many more cows than people. Locally, that's not a joke, just a fact. Outside of Alaska, Wyoming has the lowest population density of any American state. This alone made it a perfect place in a pandemic. But Wyoming turned out to be perfect for us anyway. Between the Teton and the Gros Ventre Ranges, the country is rugged, unspoiled, and as majestic as anything you could imagine. As soon as we got there, I bought a big truck—a diesel. At the Teton County clerk's office, they took my ID and came back with a set of plates that felt, to me, like the local version of "welcome."

"I bet you'll like these," the clerk said.

I did when I looked at the numbers. They read, "666."

Some days, I'd drive down to Ace Hardware or out to the bait and tackle in town. Even though I was a stranger, no one made a fuss about my jet-black hair and tattoos. I'd forget myself, talking to actual people after the weeks spent locked down in LA. Courtney would text me a few hours later: "Where are you?"

"I'm out night fishing."

When I got home, she'd ask me, "Who were you fishing with? We haven't been here a month!"

Well, I'd been fishing with guys I met down at the fly-fishing store. Fishing guides. They didn't care who I was. They just cared about what we were catching and shooting the breeze in between.

On the road, my band had driven through Wyoming. We'd gone through Montana and Idaho, Utah, Colorado. We'd done a tour once called Dead of Winter in Canada, and we had driven forever across Canada in the winter. It was eerie and desolate and beautiful, but I  don't recall ever stopping. A band like Mötley Crüe can't play small towns. Much as we'd like to, the numbers don't work. We have to play places where we can draw thousands of people. In the cities, I'd take a notebook and camera and find the places where people are struggling. Skid rows. Areas with high concentrations of drug users, prostitutes, sometimes gang members. Most of the people I talked to let me take their photos. I listened to stories, dug into the fabric that informed my songs. Those were my roots. Places I'd been myself. It was important that I stay connected to them. But I had spent so much time in the cities that it took me a while to see all the ways the country had stayed with me too. The Snake River, where I was fishing, runs past Twin Falls and Jerome, Idaho. A lifetime ago, I had lived in both places. My grandfather and I had fished the same river for salmon and steelhead. We hunted beside the banks, camped by the water. I had gotten so far from Idaho, and I'd been gone for so long—it had been ages since I had looked back, but now that I did, I was taken aback by how close it all seemed.

Maybe I hadn't gone so far away after all.

The house we bought backs onto a gulch. Where the land drops down, herds of elk come out to wander and graze. Someday, I'll build a bench there. For now, I make do with a rock. I'll sit for ten minutes, or twenty, and I'll have forgotten myself when the phone starts to ring. When I reach for it, the sight of my own hand startles me. The tattoos are familiar, but the skin's not. It's thinner, more wrinkled, translucent. When I scrape my knuckles, they take longer to heal. When I get up, my bones creak. But if the phone doesn't ring, I'll keep sitting. Watching the elk, I'll remember the Idaho farmland and flatland stretching out way beyond the horizon. I'll remember myself as a boy.

At thirteen, at home in my grandparents' double-wide trailer, I listened to records my uncle had sent from Los Angeles. Albums by Wings, Sweet, April Wine, and the Beach Boys. The songs on those records seemed much more vivid—more real—than anything Jerome had to offer. The town had one traffic light. One movie theater. One park the size of a postage stamp where the "bad" kids went to smoke.

I didn't smoke, didn't drink. I had seen drugs—to an extent, I had grown up around them—but not since my mother had sent me away. I was the new kid in town; in the fall I'd be the new kid in school yet again. When lunchtime came, I wouldn't know where to sit. I wasn't Nikki Sixx yet, I was still Frankie Feranna, and in Idaho, there weren't too many people with vowels at the end of their names.

The days dragged on and on in Jerome. Crops grew, the cows got milked, and nothing else happened. The world I heard on those songs on my uncle's LPs moved so swiftly, I was afraid I'd get left behind. Every night, I scoured the photos and lyrics and liner notes, looking for clues that would get me there quickly. But in the morning, I woke up and things were exactly the same.

If I could go back in time, I'd tell myself to slow down—even though I know I wouldn't have listened.

Q: What does it take to get you to stop moving?
A: Fifty years and a pandemic.

My older children flew up to Wyoming. They all had lives of their own, and they arrived one by one. I picked them up at the airport, took them out hiking or fishing. When they were all here, we cooked together, ate dinner together, watched movies together. In California, we'd gathered for birthdays and holidays. But we were together now for weeks on end. On the news, there was so much fear and suffering that it made this extra time we had been given feel all the more valuable.

In those first months of the pandemic, when our internal clocks had gone out of sorts in weird ways we couldn't explain, we'd talk about time itself. It was hard to remember where we'd been the previous summer, but summers we'd long since forgotten were suddenly fresh in our minds. Every once in a while, I found myself picking up the phone to call my grandparents. A year earlier, I couldn't have told you the number. Now, for some reason, I knew it again.

Of course, Nona and Tom were both dead now. Both of my parents had died. Uncle Don, who had sent me those records when I was in Idaho, died just before the pandemic got started. Don's second wife—my mother's sister Sharon—had passed on as well.

Out of those two generations, only my mom's other sister, Harlene, was still living. She and her husband, my uncle Bob, were my last links to that part of the past.

On the other side of my family, there was no one at all I could think of. My half-brother Randy. Years earlier, I'd gotten his number and called to ask him about the old man. But I had outlived Randy too.

I thought about what he'd told me: "Our father was not a good man."

In Los Angeles, Courtney had been working on our family tree. She tracked down old documents—census records, death certificates—and matched them to photos we had or managed to dig up online. We put them all into an album we planned to pass on to our daughter. But even paired to the photographs, those facts and figures only told part of the story.

Who were these people *really*? What drove them to make the decisions they'd made? How had those decisions shaped me? How were they going to shape my children in turn?

My father walked out on his family. Well into adulthood, the thought of him made me see red. But most of what I knew about him, I knew from my mother—and my mother had been her own can of worms.

I had never really forgiven either of them.

That didn't matter to them anymore. But to a surprising degree, it still mattered to me.

All my life, I had judged them—even though I'd made my own share of piss-poor decisions. I hate to say it and take no pride in it, but I'd gone through two marriages and two divorces before meeting Courtney. For all the people who stayed in my life, so many others were gone. A lot of them, I'd cut out coldly. I never abandoned my kids or made any of them feel unloved. But whatever coldness my father had felt when he left us, I must have had in me too. Was that something to root out and make sure I never passed on down the line?

Or was it the thing that had gotten us all those gold records and bought this beautiful house in Wyoming?

When you grow up with your parents, you look at yourself and think, "This came from my mom; that came from my dad." Maybe it works that way. Maybe it doesn't. Maybe the split's not as clear-cut as all that. For me, the point was that I had no way of knowing. I had been deprived of my *right* to know—and, over the years, that had been one more thing to resent. But spend enough days in Wyoming with your wife and children around you, and it gets hard to hold on to resentments. There's no longer that part of you that wants to judge.

But there's still that part of you that's a bit restless, still looking for answers, still tapping the floorboards to make sure you're on solid ground.

Our tour was on hold now, indefinitely. No one knew anything about the future, but everyone acted "as if": As if the pandemic were going to be over before the election. As if we were still going out on the road. As if the world was going to go back to being the way that it had been.

I had my doubts, but I didn't know anything either. I had to act "as if" too. At some point, I had to fly back to Los Angeles to take care of all the details, large and small, that had kept piling up.

The freeways were blissfully empty. I had quit riding six years earlier, but I would have given a lot for a bike. Instead, I put the top down. I love to be outside, the rush of the air. I'll always have a convertible, and I took mine on long drives. I went slowly because there was nowhere to go. Quite a few stores in my neighborhood were boarded up. The park with the lake where the little kids went—that was empty. It was like driving on a movie set, and I was reflecting on the forty years that had gone by since I'd formed the band, thinking about all the people I'd worked with and everything we had been through together—and not thinking at all about where I was going until I stopped for a red light, a block from the Walk of Fame, at the corner of Cahuenga and Selma.

This was where London, my band, had rehearsed.

London was the band I had before Mötley, and London lasted for many years after I quit. Slash and Izzy Stradlin had passed through London. Fred Coury from Cinderella and Blackie Lawless from W.A.S.P. On the Sunset Strip, it had become a bad joke: London was the band you passed through on your way to becoming famous—and everyone got to be famous, except for London itself.

Lizzie Grey, Dane Rage, and I formed London in Hollywood in 1978, after we'd been fired from Blackie's band Sister.

Dane was around—we'd stayed in touch—though he had long since sold his incredible-looking North Drums kit. But Lizzie, who had been my best friend, was gone.

Years earlier, sitting in my silver Vega at this intersection, we'd talked and talked about my plans for the band. I wanted us to be heavier. We both loved Mott the Hoople and Bowie and Queen. But I also loved the Sex Pistols and the Ramones, and I wanted to lean into that more and more. I had already written most of the songs that showed up on Mötley's first album. So I told Lizzie I wanted to talk, and I told him I was leaving.

I remember him crying. We'd already been through so much.

"I have to do this," I told him. I went on to form Mötley, while Lizzie kept going with London.

Before I saw him for the last time, we'd talked on the phone for the first time in years. He disclosed to me that he had Parkinson's, and we joked about all the things he couldn't do. He couldn't play guitar anymore and just sang. But sometimes, he said, he'd be singing, and he'd forget where he was standing. He wouldn't know where he was.

Even though I had prepared myself before our meeting, I was shocked to see him, blown away by what the disease had done.

Lizzie lived in Vegas—his wife drove him up with their daughters—and we met at a restaurant in Thousand Oaks. He couldn't have weighed more than 110 pounds. I walked with him on my arm to the bathroom, held him up from behind while he went, helped him zip up his pants, and that was the last time I saw him.

Thanks to Allen Kovac, my convertible is a Rolls. It's white with red leather—a beautiful car, but I bought it because it's the biggest car I could find where you could still take the top off. If they made a Dodge as big, I would have bought that instead. But the Rolls is what I had during the pandemic, and when I flew back to LA from Wyoming, I took it back up to Thousand Oaks, out to the restaurant where we had met.

Sitting in the front seat, I remembered the nights I'd spent sleeping in parks. I saw myself leading Lizzie outside, holding him up with his wife and children watching.

I thought, "Why him?"

Sometimes I forget myself and ask Allen: *Hey, do you think we could do this or do that?*

He always says the same thing: *You know you're a superstar, right?*

I sort of know it, and I sort of don't. I tell him to shut up, because I still see myself as an underdog. But I'm an underdog with a Rolls-Royce.

Why me and not Lizzie? We loved the same bands, we wrote songs together, we had all the same dreams, but my fate was my fate, and his fate was his.

"Band looking for a bass player. Must have chops, equipment, into Aerosmith."

That's how it started. An ad in the paper: guitar player looking for bass player to start a band. I know how it ended, and I was there for everything in between. But when I got back to Wyoming, I walked to the gulch where the elk were, sat down on my rock, and stayed until Courtney came looking for me.

Just Kids

Chapter 3

This is, literally, the boat we came in on ...

My paternal grandparents, Serafino and Frances, were born and married in Calascibetta, an ancient town in the center of Sicily, and my grandfather took this boat—the SS *Perugia*—to New York in 1906. Frances had just given birth to my uncle Carlo; the two of them arrived one month later, and they all ended up in California. Serafino worked for the American Can Company, and in 1918 (the year my father was born), they were living on Keys Street in

ANCHOR LINE'S S.S. PERUGIA

downtown San Jose—the same house they were living in thirty years later when Serafino passed away.

On my mother's side, my people had names like Caleb, Keturah, and Ezra. Names like Theodosia, Temperance, and—I am not making this up—Zerubbabel. They were pilgrims, like Simon Hoyt, who emigrated from Dorset, England, at the start of the seventeenth century and settled in the Massachusetts Bay Colony. Spellings hadn't been standardized yet, so I've also got Hights in my background and Haights and Hyatts. The Haights are my immediate maternal ancestors. They traveled west, joined the Church of Latter-day Saints, and settled in Mormon country. My grandfather, Horton Devitt Haight, was born in Utah in 1907 in a place called Antimony.

Horton was my grandmother Nona's first husband. Tom—the man I knew as my grandfather—was Nona's second.

Horton and Nona had three children: Harlene; Sharon; my mother, Deanna—the baby, the family darling. The girls were all born in Twin Falls, Idaho, and when Harlene was seven and my mother was around two, work brought the family out to California. They landed in Santa Cruz, where Horton and Nona got a divorce. Not long afterward, in 1951, Horton died.

Deanna was eleven. I have heard that she was wild even before Horton's death. My mother was beautiful and dreamy—and by all accounts, she was headstrong, determined, and impossible to control or reason with. At fourteen or fifteen, she started to run off from home. Nona wouldn't know where she had gone. She wouldn't know if Deanna was okay, or even alive. And then, at the age of nineteen, my mother turned up with my father in tow.

———

My dad joined the army four weeks before the attack on Pearl Harbor, so he must have shipped out soon afterward. He probably fought, but I wouldn't know where. At some point, while he was still in the service, he visited home and married a woman named Adeline. By the time he was discharged, in December 1945, they had been married for two years, but whether or not he had children from that first marriage is something I haven't learned either. The first forty years of his life are a mystery to me.

What I do know is that Frank Feranna was twice as old as my mother, who was nineteen on the day I was born, December 11, 1958.

In some families, I suppose, Frank's olive skin—his Sicilian background—would have been enough to cause a certain amount of embarrassment. (Can you imagine what Zerubbabel would have said?) In some families, the age difference alone would have created a scandal.

But there was something unconventional about that side of my family. Horton's father, for instance, had some run-ins with the law: embezzlement, maybe bank robbery. It's not entirely clear, but he got in some sort of trouble and spent time in prison—and when he got out of prison, he didn't go back to his family. He went out and started a new one and left ours behind.

The Haights would have known how to bear the whiff of a scandal.

Then there was the fact that Nona was older than Tom, the man she married after Horton's death—quite a bit older, by sixteen years. When Tom was little, Nona had been his babysitter. When he grew up and went into the army and was stationed at Fort Ord, on Monterey Bay, they met once again.

So age difference was nothing new either.

Or it may simply be that Nona was happy just having Deanna back all in one piece.

Whatever the case was, my mother was home again—safe, sound, and pregnant. Right away, there was a fuss about me. Mom had a few names picked out, but Frank insisted that I was going to be named after him. He must have been adamant—the way Mom talked about it in years to come, I pictured him raging and ripping things

29

Joseph P. Porter
The Pioneer Broadside
1958

off the walls—and, of course, he got his way: I became Franklin Carlton Feranna Junior. But having a son named after him wasn't enough to keep Frank Sr. at home. By the time I was old enough to understand what was happening around me, he had abandoned my mother and me.

Or so I thought for a very long time. The truth is, it's more complicated. The truth always is—in my family, at least. The truth is that Frank and Deanna had another child, a sister I never knew.

Lisa's life is a mystery too. I must have known her briefly as a baby—but that was so long ago. I was too young to remember. The first time I *really* saw Lisa, she was lying in her wooden casket. It was a child's casket because my sister, who was thirty-nine when she died, was a very small person. She was born blind and with Down syndrome. I have her church shoes now—little white shoes she had worn, once a week, for a very long time. They don't have a scuff on them because she had never been able to walk.

She had a perfect face. Unlined and angelic. Even with her eyes closed, looking at her was a bit like looking into the mirror. We looked that much alike. Standing there, in the funeral parlor, I filled up with regrets. The night before, I'd called my mother, and she and I had had one of our terrible conversations.

"Why didn't I meet her? Why didn't we ever visit?"

"We couldn't see her," my mother said. "It made her very upset when we did."

But at the funeral parlor, I met a man whose parents had cared for my sister.

"That's not true," he told me. "She knew about you and loved you and missed you, and she would ask about you."

Other things my mother had told me couldn't have possibly been true—starting with her middle name: Lisa Maria. According to Mom, my sister had been named for Elvis's daughter. But Lisa Marie Presley was born in 1968; Lisa Maria Feranna was born in 1960.

That's not a big deal—a tiny lie or a thing misremembered. But if it *was* a lie, could I trust anything else I'd been told about Lisa? Thinking about it reminds me of something my aunt Harlene has to say: "Your mother and I never fought. She and your aunt Sharon got along too. The three of us got along fine, other than the fact that your mother did not tell the truth—about anything."

Here's a recipe, in case you want to make your own rock star at home:

* Take a child. The more impressionable and imaginative the better.
* Add a dash of neglect or abuse and a generous sprinkling of abandonment.
* If you have other siblings on hand, subject them to the same treatment, and let the child see.
* Shake vigorously, and let sit.

It's a rough formula; I'm sure there are others. But from what I've seen in my time in the rock-and-roll trenches, that one's a good starting place.

In my case, I've done the math. It looks like this: Lisa was born on November 11, one month, to the day, before my second birthday. According to what I've learned since her death, she stayed with us for another ten months. Long enough for me to get to know her and love her. Long enough to mark her absence. As far as I could have possibly understood it, one day my sister had just . . . disappeared. Who was to say the same thing couldn't happen to me?

And, of course, Lisa's disappearance didn't occur in a vacuum; my father had disappeared too.

Joseph P. Porter
The Pioneer Woodside
1918

Throughout my childhood, I imagined that Frank had abandoned us after my birth. Obviously, I was wrong. He was around at the start of 1960, when my mother got pregnant again. He was around in November, when Lisa was born. And he was still around, ten months later, when Lisa was taken to live with the family who ended up caring for her.

That wasn't the story I'd grown up hearing.

When I asked Harlene about it, I was surprised that she and her husband, Bob—who was there at the time and is still there today—had fond memories of my father.

"Frank was handsome," Aunt Harlene said.

"He was a very talented artist," said Uncle Bob.

Harlene and Bob are in their eighties now. They live in Idaho, and during the first year of COVID-19, I wasn't able to see them at all—but I loved speaking with them on the phone. They were both sharp as tacks, and after sixty-some years of marriage, they'd turned their old habit of finishing each other's sentences into an art form.

"All the stuff you've heard about him is wrong—"

"Well, Bob, we don't know that."

"We know he was a really good person, really talented, really—"

"We really liked him."

"Your parents would come over and visit with us," Bob said. "We had a new house with a beautiful patio built in the back, with benches, raised flower beds, all sorts of stuff. Your father designed all of that. I can't recall what he did for a living. He must have been an architect. He could pick up a pencil and paper and draw anything in the world. Anything you would have wanted."

"We really were fond of him," Aunt Harlene said.

"Did you know anything about his background? Do you recall anything about his family?"

"Not a bit. He didn't talk about that."

"Do you know why he and my mother split up?"

"Something happened that made him really mad," Bob said, "because we never saw him again. At the time, we assumed Deanna did something, and he didn't like it."

"Maybe she did," Harlene added. "Don't know."

Mystery, unsolved. Someone did something. *Something* must have happened. But even if Bob and Harlene had known, at some point, what that something had been, they weren't telling. Or—because they're direct, honest people—they had blocked that thing out or forgotten. There'd been a long line of guys after Frank. Some they knew about; some they didn't. ("She didn't last long with anybody," Harlene says. "Frank was probably the one she stayed with the longest.")

My mother's life was a lot to keep straight. But that doesn't make me less curious about what *did* happen.

I can't imagine what it was like, bringing my sister home from the hospital. As I understand it, she wasn't expected to live. Anyone would have been overwhelmed. Any marriage would have been strained to the breaking point. When Lisa did not die and they gave her up—how do you get over that?

What if you don't? What if you shut down? What if my mother was shut down already?

"Was my mother affectionate with me?" I asked Aunt Harlene.

"I really can't say. I know that when you were born and brought home from the hospital, I came down to the apartment where Deanna lived with your dad. I stayed for two weeks and took care of you—she didn't want to—and I didn't think much about it. She loved to cook, and she knew I loved babies and kids, so both of us were in our element. Now that I'm older, I realize I should have made her care for you and bond with you. But I was a kid myself. What do kids know?"

Maybe my father didn't abandon us. Maybe my mother drove him away.

But it's easy to blame the mother.

Take the fight over my naming. Maybe that story had been backward too.

Maybe my father—proud Sicilian man that he was—was full of joy to have been borne a son. Maybe that story wasn't so much about anger on his part as pride.

Then again, maybe it wasn't. Maybe his fist had left holes in a wall.

And even if Deanna had tried to stop Frank from calling or visiting me (I don't think she did, but let's say she did, for argument's sake), it would have been no excuse.

"Something happened that made him really mad, because we never saw him again," Bob had said.

But Frank never saw me again either.

Nona and Tom

W e bounced around after that: Lake Tahoe, Reno, El Paso. We seem to have never stayed in one place for too long.

Bob and Harlene were the first to move out to Lake Tahoe. By trade, Bob was an automotive machinist. He spent thirteen years working for a company in Santa Cruz, and then he struck out on his own after learning that Tahoe had an auto parts store without a machine shop attached. He and Harlene moved out to set up that shop, and for many years, it was the only machine shop in town.

My grandfather, Tom, was a machinist and auto mechanic, like Bob. He and Nona followed Bob and Harlene out to Tahoe, and Tom got a job at the shop.

At some point, we must have joined them.

Deanna got a job as a dealer—blackjack—at Harvey's Wagon Wheel. It wasn't where she wanted to be. She had dreamed of becoming a model or an actress. She was drawn to musicians and show business types. But the casino floor wasn't too far from the stage, and after hours she got to mingle with the entertainers. She'd stay out all night, sneaking home in the morning. Once in a while, I'd wake up and there would be a strange man in our apartment. I was young, but there's one person I remember especially well, both because he stuck around for a while and because there was something unusual about him. A few unusual things, actually. He was kind, and I remember him down on his hands and knees, playing with me, cracking jokes that I thought were the funniest things in the world. He had held on to his own inner child but would sometimes be sad. I'd climb up onto the couch, put my head on his shoulder.

If he'd been gone for a while and showed up suddenly, he'd see me and beam. "Frankie, my man!"

Richard would come to town for a few weeks and leave, but he always came back. I was always thrilled to see him. But not everyone felt the same way.

It was the sixties, but not the late sixties. Men still wore hats. Miscegenation—"marriage and/or sexual relations between the races"—was still illegal in several states. Fifteen years earlier, it had been illegal in California, and it was still very much frowned upon. Deanna lost her job at Harvey's. The pit bosses told her it was against the rules for casino-floor workers to date entertainers, but I'm sure there were other things they couldn't stand. At that time, that kind of relationship was rare, if not unheard of.

If I know anything about my mother, I'm sure that we had been living from paycheck to paycheck. We wouldn't have had any savings. Our only safety net would have been family—and that must have been a big help, with the hours my mother worked and all the time she spent out on the town—but nobody had any money. I didn't know it at the time, but looking back now, I realize that we really had nothing. Losing the job would have been a real blow. I don't know how she felt at the time about losing Richard. Later on, Mom must have had her regrets, although, if she did, she didn't speak about them. It was only when I got much older that I put two and two together and realized, "*Ohhhh . . . Richard Pryor.*"

But, like my dad, Richard disappeared, and I don't know that it was by choice. According to Bob and Harlene, he kept calling my mother. When she refused his calls, he called them. It took Richard a while to give up, and it took him a while to become truly famous. But by the time I entered high school, he'd become more than famous—he was an icon. No one in Jerome would ever have believed he had dated my mother. I could have just as easily told them we'd spent a year living with aliens. Up in Idaho, California seemed like some other world.

———

My mother found work at other casinos, but nothing as steady as her job at Harvey's had been. Before long, she started to disappear too. She'd be gone for long stretches of time, or what seemed like long stretches to me. I stayed with Nona and Tom or shuttled between them and Bob and Harlene. I must have started school there, in Tahoe, but whatever memories I have are hopelessly mixed in with memories of other schools in other places. Mostly, I recall the outdoors. Swimming during the summer. Riding around on snowmobiles when it snowed. I would have been too small to drive one, so I was probably sitting on Bob's lap or Tom's—and Bob and Harlene had their kids, who were my older cousins. It must have been snowing on the day that I did see my dad one last time. I would have been about four—I know that because I once had a photo of us from that day—and he gave me a little red saucer, a sled. I remembered it the other day in Wyoming, when I went to Ace Hardware to get my daughter a sled. Outside, the snow was coming down hard. It was just pounding, I came out the door with the same sort of red saucer for Ruby, and it hit me hard, this memory of my father that I still cherish because it's the only real memory of him that I have. But except for missing him and missing Richard, I don't recall being too sad in Tahoe, or lonely. My cousins and I spent so much time together, they felt like siblings to me. Bob and Harlene were always around, Nona and Tom. Those were good times, surrounded by family.

Tom was extremely outdoorsy, like a frontiersman born into the wrong century. He loved to fish and hunt, and if there was some tool he needed to finish a task, he could sit down and fashion it himself. I was intrigued by his tools—they were like toys you could use to make other toys. I was obsessed with his pocketknife. I wanted one like it, and Tom bought me one I kept for a long time. I didn't know he'd sold off some of his tools to buy it. Those were tools he used to make his living, but his first thought had been, "Frankie wants this. What can I sell?" It's funny to think that he ended up stuck in an office. But before that happened, my mom reappeared, and she and I and her new boyfriend, Bernie, went on a great big adventure down to Puerto Vallarta.

Bernie was a musician, a trumpet player who played, on and off, with Frank Sinatra. Maybe, for Mom, he was a step up from Richard. But for some reason, I was scared of him. Today, I'm more inclined to give Bernie some leeway. As a musician, he wasn't getting off work until well after midnight—and what do kids do in the morning? Ruby starts kicking and screaming and watching cartoons, and I'm sure I did the same thing. It was the last thing that Bernie needed to hear in the morning, having stayed up half the night. As an adult, I have a better understanding of where he might have been coming from. But all I ever heard from him then was, "Be quiet, be quiet!"

It was a bummer to deal with, and I'm sure I was a bummer for him. But there I was, so he gave me a hard time, nonstop. He didn't like the way I slouched down in my chair. He didn't like it when I put my elbows on the kitchen table. He didn't like the way I brushed my teeth, side to side and not up and down, like he'd taught me. He didn't like it when I woke him up, so he would yell at me, and I'd think, "You aren't my dad."

I don't think I said it out loud. Once, Bernie hit me or slapped me—I had been brushing my teeth the wrong way, yet again—and that turned into a violent fight between him and my mother. Tons

of screaming with me sitting on the floor, crying after getting my mouth smacked. Even then, I don't think I said anything out loud.

Here's a photo of the three of us then. It looks like Bernie and my mom have been drinking wine as well as coffee. Smoking too: Marlboro Reds. But although they're relaxed, Bernie's still off to the side, his arms crossed. Mom's are open; she seems to be eying me with real love, but she's not reaching for me or sitting all that close. To me, she looks like a woman who's being pulled in two different directions—which, I am sure, was the case. And Bernie—well, Bernie looks like a man who's not my father.

But Bernie must have tolerated me to some extent if he agreed to take me down to Mexico. It's not entirely clear to me why he and my mom wanted to go. Bob thinks it's because it would have been easier for them to buy property in Mexico if my mom gave birth in Mexico. (In any case, it didn't happen. My sister Celia was born in the States.) I don't think I knew Deanna was pregnant. All I knew then was that, one day, we just packed up and went.

The trip down wasn't too comfortable. Bernie had a small car—a Corvair or a Karmann Ghia. He had a big dog, a mean German shepherd, and the two of us were scrunched up in the back, where Bernie and my mom had also stowed all the stuff they hadn't been able to fit in the trunk. The dog bit. She snarled. When we stopped and got out, she chased me. The roads we were driving on were all dirt roads, and at one point we got stuck in a creek. A river had overflowed and filled a part of the road that dipped down just a bit. It wasn't the best thing for a sports car with three people and too much stuff. But when people got out of their own cars to push us, the dog started snarling and barking at them. The whole trip had been a small nightmare already. But it was worth it because, when we got there, Puerto Vallarta turned out to be the most magical place.

I was born by a Pacific bay, but the Bahía de Banderas was very different from the Bay Area. Tropical. Lush. Everywhere you turned, there were lizards—and lizards were magical too. Our little house was one hundred steps up the side of a mountain, and every couple of steps, there'd be something to see. There were donkeys and iguanas. From the top of the mountain, you looked down and saw all the animals and then the ocean itself. I'd stare out for hours, watching the boats go by, and, more than ever before, I was allowed to wander. I'd run down the steps, play with other kids on the beach, and swim and run around naked. There were street vendors cooking corn wrapped in aluminum foil with cilantro and butter and salt that you'd eat on a stick, and I got a tapeworm from eating ceviche—though that was another thing I found out later. Back in the States, I went to the bathroom and then called for Nona. I thought my intestines were coming out, and I was terrified. I had to go to the hospital and stay overnight. They didn't feed me and gave me Epsom salts to starve the tapeworm out. I got to experience my first hospital bedpan. That ended up being one more thing to hold against Bernie. But there's only one thing Bernie did that I don't understand.

Our house was very small. We didn't have a TV, but we'd have people over. I have faint memories of Bernie and my mother drinking and smoking weed, although I didn't know what weed was at the time. And I have some memories of Bernie asking me if I wanted to try what he was smoking. I recall doing that and feeling kind of tripped out, and it wasn't until much later that I realized he'd turned me on to marijuana, and I wasn't even seven years old.

Parents did things then that they would be put in jail for today. It was the sixties. You'd go to somebody's house, and they'd be naked. The grown-ups were naked. Kids never wore clothes at all. Grown-ups did messed-up things, and you'd feel frightened, but you would roll with the punches. It bothered me more much later in life, when it allowed me to do what I'm so good at doing: saying, "Fuck that guy. Fuck him. Look at him now." Bernie certainly helped give me my shitty attitude toward people who'd done me wrong.

Courtney says that if anyone treats me with disrespect, I come unhinged. That's true to this day. You cannot put your hands on me. You are not allowed to disrespect me. My boundaries are set. Even a small thing can burn a relationship, and if I'm angry enough, I don't mind burning myself to burn you.

But Puerto Vallarta. The smells and the colors. There was an old shipwreck that had been left out to rot. To me, it was the coolest thing that had ever existed. When I first got clean from heroin, I went back to Puerto Vallarta. It wasn't a return to the scene of the crime; it was more like squaring the circle. I didn't have a girlfriend. I only had one clean friend, and he and I spent all our time on the beach. We'd lie out there and talk, and for me, it was the start of a much better life—the start of the life I have now.

You might think that when you get clean, life swells up into big bowls of cherries. But the opposite happens. When you get off drugs or whatever Band-Aids you've been using to cover your wounds, you start to hurt and ask hard questions. If you haven't said, "I'm going to do this one day at a time and turn my life over to some higher power," you're in for a hell of a ride. I really plugged into AA at that time. I surrounded myself with people who were healthy and sober and had things they wanted to live for. I've always believed in surrounding myself with people who are smarter than me and better than me at whatever I'm wanting to do. Hopefully I can bring something to the party that's more than my name or my notoriety. At the least, I believe, I'll learn some things and have some useful humility beat into me. And I'll always associate Mexico with good things, even if Bernie was not one of them.

I try not to take it too personally. Bernie was a shitty dad to Celia too—hardly around—and Celia was his flesh and blood and a wonderful person, so I don't think it was me, specifically, that he objected to. The man hated kids, and he shouldn't have had them. What that meant, ultimately, was that he and my mother were not meant to be. But by the time they finally broke up for good, I was gone. I had already gone back to living with Nona and Tom.

We lived in Carson Valley now, just south of Reno. A new highway was in the works that went over the Donner Pass. Tom had been hired by one of the crews as a welder. He worked on the equipment until that highway was finished and then teamed up with a man who convinced him to go into business, setting up a firm that sold all kinds of insurance. I have vague memories of them doing it. Mark Twain Insurance, the company was called. By this point, we'd moved to Yerington, Nevada—a dry desert town an hour and a half outside of Reno. It seemed like an unlikely place to be selling insurance, but Tom and his partner kept the business going for a year, maybe more, until some government agency took notice. Apparently, they'd been selling insurance policies that didn't have proper backing—nothing illegal, but enough to get them in some sort of jam. They sold their contracts to one of the big national companies.

Tom wasn't cut out for office life, after all. But he and Nona had just enough money left to start again. That's how we ended up living in Texas and New Mexico.

After a year in the office, Tom probably wanted to go back to working with his hands outdoors. That didn't happen right away—and when it did, it may not have been all that he'd hoped for—but it did happen, eventually. First, he got a job fixing cars at a Shell Station in El Paso.

My grandmother and I would visit him there. I remember the smell of grease, and I remember that I loved it. It felt like I was part of a secret club, full of cool guys with slicked-back hair and toys they worked on all day and into the night, until each one was perfect. Hot rods were a big thing in those days, all-American muscle, and I thought that Shell Station was the Taj Mahal. At home, I built models. But my grandfather worked on real cars. He changed real tires. He rebuilt real motors. It was fascinating. And you would think it would have carried over to me—but no. The only tool I've ever learned how to use is my bass.

A lot of Texas is windswept, but this part was also especially hot, with no lakes that I knew of to go swimming in. But we had moved to a little house that was next door to a grade school, so there was a baseball field and a football field, and if you looked straight across the street, you'd see the house where my friend Juan lived. The door was always open, and Juan's mom was always cooking. She fed us, and when we went over to my house, Nona fed us.

We rode our bikes to the park. There was a ball field there too. The older neighborhood kids played, and Juan and I hung on the chain link and watched. Afterward, when all the big kids had gone, we looked for lost baseballs—prized possessions in our jacket pockets as we rode our Schwinn Stingrays home.

Juan had a small house, and ours was small too. All the houses in our neighborhood were small, square houses, but Juan and I didn't know that they were small at the time. They were same-looking houses with two or three bedrooms, and no one had swimming pools. They just had little backyards that bumped up to the neighbors' backyards, side yards that bumped up against side yards, with shared fences. Everyone must have known their neighbors' business. But for a small kid, a little backyard was enough. There was a front yard too, where you could leave your bikes. They were old bikes that didn't have gears or kickstands. You'd throw them right down on the grass, and if you forgot to come back and get them, they'd still be sitting there, no matter how many hours had passed. Life was gentler then, more innocent. We put playing cards through the spokes of our wheels to make our bikes sound like they had racing engines. After chores, we'd save our pennies and nickels and spend them on Black Cat firecrackers, which were legal in Texas. Piggly Wiggly was the place to go, the big hangout for us because they had models and Hot Wheels.

There was one model Juan and I built together. A long dragster with big wheels in the back, tiny wheels in the front, and a gigantic spoiler. We spent a long time on the paint, the decals—the model was a big deal, and it had pride of place in my bedroom until, one day, Juan and I took it out into the yard. We took a whole pack of firecrackers, taped it to the side of the model, and blew the thing up.

My grandmother heard us, of course. She came out and said, "How could you do that?" But life was so simple, when blowing up a model was the worst thing you could possibly do.

Sometimes Juan and I made jumps out of cinder blocks and plywood. Ramps, right in the center of our street, and cars that came down the street slowed down and carefully went around us. Sometimes we slept out in the yard, staying up late, looking at the stars. When we moved to New Mexico, I was heartbroken. I had lost my best friend.

———

In Anthony, we lived in a trailer with a septic tank out in the back, a propane tank, and a giant pile of dirt where the septic tank had been dug out. I played on that mound and made mud slides whenever it rained—amazing desert rains, where the whole country flash-flooded and *everything* turned into mud.

I spent a long time on those slides. I really focused. Something about them sparked my imagination. I'd lose myself for hours. Eventually, Nona came out and snapped me out of whatever world I'd been creating. On the farm, there was just too much to do.

When I say "farm," you might picture fields full of corn or cabbage—in other words, crops. This wasn't that kind of farm. If we'd had horses, you'd call it a ranch. But we had hogs, so it was a farm—a hog farm. There wasn't much green stuff around. Two or three hundred yards down the road, we had a fenced-off area where the pigs slopped and slept. We had a donkey named Gabe, a small pony (I don't know why we had a pony), and rabbits, which I had to feed. We had chickens—fetching the eggs was another chore I had been given—and a psychotic rooster that attacked me whenever I so much as peeked into the coop. I hated that thing as much as I'd hated Bernie's German shepherd, and I complained constantly until the day Tom pulled up in his El Camino. I looked in the back and saw the rooster lying there with no head. I was happy and grateful. But Nona and Tom got their money's worth out of me. I slopped the pigs. I dug the holes for fence posts. I went out with tools, even though I was terrible with tools, and mended the barbed-wire fence.

Picture a barbed-wire fence with regular fence posts, like you'd see out in the country. There'd be a hinged gate you could open to step into the pen or corral.

Well, we didn't have regular fence posts—what we had looked more like tree trunks or stumps—and we didn't have a hinged gate. We just had the barbed wire, and in order to close the pen, you had to take a post, pull the wire until it was taut, and hook a loop of barbed wire over the post so that the tension held the fence together. When those loops came undone, I'd go fix them, and when I was done with my chores, I'd hang out with the animals.

I didn't mind those chores at all, now that the rooster was dead. It would be blistering hot—I didn't care. It would be raining, but I wouldn't care. I'd lie down beside one of the pigs, prop my back and my head against the pig's side, and look up at the stars. I thought the pigs were my friends. The rabbits were too, until I discovered that another of my chores was to kill them. We ate those rabbits for supper, and that was disturbing. It's *still* disturbing, remembering the two-by-four Tom had carved into a weapon like a baseball bat, complete with a grip. But I can see now that I was being taught a lesson: What we killed, we had to eat. What we ate, we had to kill.

Tom was trying to teach me the true cost of things.

It was the same with the pigs. A truck would come rattling down our dirt road, and my friends, the pigs, would get taken away. We'd be left with the piglets. When the piglets grew up, the truck came back again.

That was the circle of farming, the circle of life. It wasn't all sunshine and flowers.

———————

In Anthony, most of the roads were dirt roads. There was an old woman who lived in a trailer right across the dirt road from ours. She was always drinking something, always smoking while talking in her raspy voice—she should have been frightening and really was a bit ghoulish, but she was interesting to me. The lines on her face, her stories, the ashes that fell down from her cigarettes, her dog lying out on the dirt porch were all interesting.

Quite a way farther on down the road was a stop for the school bus. I don't believe it was marked or was much more than the corner of one dirt road meeting another, but there were three or four more trailers there. Older kids lived in those trailers, and they messed with me, every day, on the bus. They stole the lunch Nona had made for me out of my lunch box or made me give them my lunch money.

One day they pushed me down to the floorboard, put their feet on top of me, and held me down for the half hour it took for the bus to go over those dirt roads and get to the school. It was dirty and dusty and sweaty—there was no air-conditioning—and something boiled over in me.

"That's the last time *that's* going to happen," I said to myself.

I let it go that day, but I didn't forget. As soon as I left the house the next day, I dumped my lunch in the bushes and filled the lunch box with rocks. The moment I got on the bus, the older kids started in. They didn't feel bad. If anything, they were emboldened. There wasn't much I could do. But as soon as we got off the bus, I called out the name of one of the older kids. He turned around, and I hit him in the face with the lunch box as hard as I could. He hit the ground right away, and I swung for the other older kid. There was blood on the lunch box, blood on my clothes, blood all over the older kids' faces—but it didn't end there, because I was taken straight down to the principal's office.

I recall feeling proud of myself. My lunch box was sitting there, right on the principal's desk. It had a new dent next to the STP sticker Tom had brought home for me from the Shell Station, and I was proud of how that dent had gotten there. I felt like I had really achieved something—and I really had. None of the bigger kids would ever dare to mess with me again.

"These kids were picking on me," I told the principal.

"You can't hit people, Frankie."

"But these kids were picking on me."

In the end, they called Tom to come down. He heard the principal out, and he said, "Okay, I'll straighten him out."

I thought I was going to be in so much trouble. But when I got into the El Camino, Tom put his arm around me.

"I'm really proud of you," he said.

I never forgot that. When my son Decker was in the fifth grade, he did the same thing. Decker was always a self-contained kid. He always kept to himself and would never have messed with another kid the way those older kids had messed with me. But when Decker makes his mind up to do something, it's going to get done. One day he was minding his own business, and a group of kids started throwing rocks in his direction.

I got a call from the principal's office fifteen minutes later. I lived a block from the school, and when I got there, I understood right away what had happened. Decker had beaten the shit out of five older kids.

I took him home, and as soon as we got inside, I put my arm around him.

"I'm really proud of you," I said.

If you walked for what seemed like a couple of miles past that bus stop in Anthony, you'd come to a convenience store housed in a shack. Here in Wyoming, it's buildings and barns. Real big barns. In Anthony, all the houses were makeshift—adobe meets plywood meets cinder blocks and aluminum siding. Most of the town was Hispanic, and all my friends were Latino. I still have my class picture from that year—1969—and I'm one of the few white kids in a sea of brown faces. It wasn't foreign to me. I had lived in Mexico. I had lived in El Paso—we'd gone into Juárez all the time. I felt a deep connection to that old Catholic culture and probably would have been happy there if we had stayed. But our farm wasn't the moneymaker Tom hoped it would be.

My grandmother was always Tom's partner in crime, and once in a while she'd work outside the home—at one time, she and Harlene worked together in a hair salon. But Nona mostly stayed at home. She had to because she had to take care of me, and Tom worked several jobs. Even after we moved out to Anthony, he drove

back and forth to the Shell Station—not much more than thirty miles, but those dirt roads weren't easy. He left early and came home late, and when he wasn't working out there, he'd be working at home. I can see now what I didn't see then: all their lives, Nona and Tom chased paychecks and chased jobs, trying to take care of me and each other.

The Shell Station must have been why we moved back to El Paso instead of going elsewhere when the farm failed to pan out.

El Paso was where the work was.

I was excited to move back to Texas. When we ended up four blocks away from Juan's house, I couldn't believe it. I walked over there right away and got Juan, and we walked past the grade school toward the junior high school, but I recall thinking that something had changed. We were different, and I hadn't even been gone very long. I remember coming back home that day, feeling like I didn't have a best friend anymore, plopping down to watch TV and sulk.

At that time, television programming was based around old-fashioned ideas about American life. Soap operas until school let out, followed by a couple of hours devoted to kid shows: *The Munsters. Batman. Gilligan's Island.* Looking back now, it's easy to picture those network executives, sitting in some office out in Burbank—"Kids between twelve and fifteen like *The Munsters*"—and think, "Oh, no. I really got caught in the system!" But sometimes being caught in the system feels great. TV was a great tranquilizer—I don't remember it being too long before I got over the end of my friendship with Juan—and school wasn't much of a drag yet. School was where all the books were, and I've always been able to lose myself in a good book. School was where all the art supplies were. School was where the girls were.

Our move back to El Paso also coincided with the start of my interest in girls. There was a house behind ours that was just like our house with a family just like our family—except for the girl who lived there. I'd see her sunbathing in her backyard, and I couldn't believe it. On school days, I tried to leave the house early to get to the corner before she arrived. That way, I'd be cool and composed when she got there. But I didn't really know how to be cool. I had no moves. I didn't have any courage. If I had opened my mouth—even if I had just said, "Hey, I'm Frankie. We're neighbors."—it would have come out all wrong. So I stood there like a lump.

Later on, when I had my first band, the other guys teased me about it: they'd be hitting on girls while I stood there, leaning against the back wall like a lump. But for that time and place, it was the right strategy. I always ended up with more girls or the prettiest girls at the end of the night. But I *did* have a band by that point. I had swagger. In Texas, as far as girls were concerned, I might as well have been a tumbleweed or a cactus. But we weren't meant for Texas anyway. Tom wanted more than his job at the Shell had to offer, and even though Anthony hadn't worked out, Nona and Tom held on to their hopes and dreams, and they carried us back to the part of the country the family had come from. No one asked me about it, but that's not surprising, and I didn't mind. I would have gone anywhere with Nona and Tom.

Twin Falls

Chapter 5

We never slept in hotels. To get us from Tahoe to Texas, we had piled into a U-Haul. When we stopped for the night, Tom put a sleeping bag out by the side of the truck. I slept stretched out on the floorboard, Nona lay across the bench seats, and Tom slept out under the stars. In the morning, we'd get up, have coffee and donuts, and get back on the road. We rented a U-Haul to move out to Anthony too—though that was a straight shot with no sleeping involved. We had a U-Haul for the move back to El Paso. And when we moved up to Idaho, Tom went and rented a U-Haul again.

But maybe it wasn't so simple. At some point, I am sure, I went back and lived with my mother—not in Lake Tahoe but in Hollywood. In fact, I *know* I did because I remember the model shop, which was a block or two up from our house.

Later on, we lived in Topanga Canyon—that was a bit like Anthony or El Paso, all woodsy and scrubby and dry. But down by the model shop, the city was dense, with tons of street life and traffic—trucks, buses, cars. If I were to guess, I'd say that we had landed in Hollywood. But wherever we were, there were a million man-made things to look at, and I tried to take in as much as I could on the way to the store. At that age, every trip out of the house can feel like an adventure—an endless emotional rush. Every picket fence post on the way. Each street you have to cross. Every group of strangers you have to walk by or step around to get through the model shop's door—and once you're inside, you're overcome with the awe, the excitement. I'd get lost in the store's narrow aisles and come out, blinking, into the sunshine. Sometimes I'd have enough money to get the same kind of dragster I'd built and blown up with Juan. But what I really wanted was a big pop-pop boat.

A pop-pop boat is a brilliant invention: a simple steam-powered toy with a boiler and two exhausts. It can be powered with a candle or a tiny burner full of vegetable oil. The kind that my model shop sold was powered with pellets, and my mom finally bought one for me. I played with it for hours, watching it putter slowly from one side of our swimming pool to the other. Sometimes it ran out of "gas," and I'd have to go into the water to get it, and that was an adventure in itself.

Our swimming pool was in the center of the apartment complex Mom had moved into, but no one else ever used it. I don't know why. It wasn't dirty; the complex was actually nice, with two stories, exterior stairs that led up to wraparound balconies, and creamish-tan stucco walls. We lived in one of the first-floor apartments at the very end of one of the rectangles that made up the complex. Inside, we had a space-age sectional sofa and shag carpeting. Many years later, when our *Girls, Girls, Girls* album came out, I bought a ranch-style house in a place called Hidden Hills, and the first thing I did was put in green shag carpeting.

All my friends were aghast. "How could you do that?"

Well, I could do it because I loved that kind of carpeting. You never see it anymore, but in 1987, it brought back good memories of that first time I lived in LA.

We had a sound system too, with gigantic speakers, and Mom played Motown and Latin music while she cooked. She cooked nonstop at the time because we always had people there, drinking cocktails, smoking jazz cigarettes—and Mom would be drinking and smoking weed too. She didn't feel like a mom. She was just one more cool person in this cool place with cool food and good music. Of course, she got me out of bed too. Combed my hair, cooked me breakfast, sent me off to school. But I don't remember the school, just the smell of the things she'd be cooking: lasagna or menudo (a kind of Mexican soup), ten feet away from the room where the hip people were and the cool music was playing.

The hip people were probably entertainers or musicians—those were the people my mother was drawn to—and friends of whoever she would have been dating. Two of them, Carl and Alan, were professional football players. They were gigantic, the biggest men I'd ever seen. To me, they were both tall as houses, and when they carried me around on their shoulders, I felt tall enough to touch the sun, singled out—more than special, because I knew that, out on the field, Carl and Alan were monsters. They even had monster-like names, which I loved: along with two other players on their team, the Vikings, they were known as the Purple People Eaters.

At that time, the Purple People Eaters were the most feared defensive line in the NFL.

Carl was a defensive end. Alan played defensive tackle. Together, they taught me to play chess. They had all the patience in the world for me, and I've always been grateful. Whenever my band played in Minneapolis, I'd get a Minnesota Vikings jersey and put it on for the encore.

I used to get razzed for it. People would say, "We don't even like the Vikings here in Minnesota!"

I'd go, "You'll never understand."

And I don't think they would have. It was something I'd carried from way, way back. Something that meant so much to me then that I was going to carry it with me for the rest of my life. It was a loyalty thing. But no one understood the black lines under my eyes either. I could have trademarked those lines—they were as much a part of my look as David Bowie's lightning bolt was part of his. People called them war paint. But not one person I met in the eighties ever thought to connect them to football.

There was a guy on the second floor of the complex, and I've carried him with me as well. An old man, a World War II veteran, who spent all his time in his chair, with his lap covered by an old blanket. I was intrigued by him because he had a tracheostomy—a hole in his throat—and a flap that fluttered over it when he talked in his cracked, raspy voice. He loved to tell me war stories, and I loved to listen, hypnotized by him and that fluttering flap. Like the old lady in Anthony, he should have been frightening to a kid. But, like that old lady, he was just fascinating.

I didn't know at the time that I was going to end up being a writer or that I would create characters in my songs. But I was hungry for the information. I knew this stuff was useful. I knew it was fuel.

These were poems and songs, waiting and asking to be written. And when I did start writing, I'd look at other songwriters and think, "What are you all even doing?" I felt like, "What's your point, even being alive?" Singing the same stuff about nothing: "My love is a rose / and it grows"? Why had they even bothered to write those words out? I felt that I had a lot more to say, and whenever I did say something, I made sure I meant it.

I loved the scars. The tracheostomies. The war wounds. War stories. Tragedy. Heartbreak. Things that had actually happened.

I think about it like this: my job, as a songwriter, is to describe the world that I see as it is, not as I'd like it to be. Vince Neil once told me, "You look down on people." My wife once said something along the same lines: "You look down on people who were born with silver spoons." She was right: I do look down on those people. I look down on how superficial they are. On the way they don't even register suffering. It's as if other people's pain doesn't exist.

But it does exist, and you can't cut yourself off from that pain without losing a lot of good things that go with it. All the lines etched into an old person's hands and face: every one of those lines tells a story. Just looking at them, letting yourself see their beauty—that's half the work. All their hopes, all their fears, all that motivates them or maybe makes them wish they didn't exist—those are real things to write about. Not "moon/June" clichés, but true, hard objects out in the real world. They're like bricks. Clichés are clouds. It's no fun to throw clouds. But you can throw bricks through a window—and that's what a rock song should be, a thing that breaks windows.

The biggest thing that Los Angeles had going for it was my sister Celia. Ceci was a tiny thing then, with brown bangs and big eyes, and she was forever tied to my side. I felt very protective of her, and I don't know if that's tied to my feelings of having loved and lost Lisa. But it's a regret that I have, the time I didn't get to spend with either of them. For a lot of my life, I've lived in Los Angeles. But even here in Wyoming, I'm a long way from Ceci, who's spent most of her life in Seattle. I have deep, deep feelings for her. But she  ended up with our mom, and I didn't. In time, she had to care for our mom. There were stretches when I only knew what Mom was up to because I called Ceci to hear Ceci's news. No matter how off the rails my life had gone—no matter how wrapped up I'd been in myself—I always wanted to know. I never stopped feeling protective.

I had my old, dented lunch box with me in Los Angeles—I had it when my mom shipped me back to live with Nona and Tom—and I still have it today. I recall packing it, along with some clothes. I didn't have much more to pack. But there was nothing I would have needed that Nona and Tom would have been unable to provide.

They had ended up in Pocatello, Idaho—a small city built over old Shoshone land, a few miles away from Snake River. It was a bit like El Paso, small houses on small lots with sidewalks, and lots of time spent outside on my bike. A drainage ditch ran behind all the houses on our side of the street, and I recall making a ramp with some of the neighborhood kids. We rode our bikes barefoot and jumped the ditch, and one day I landed mine right in the water and felt something scrape across the bottom of my foot. That was a gnarly wound, full of white gristle, and we had to get it stitched up, but it was also another adventure. In Pocatello, the kids didn't go home until the sun started to set. You had your bike and your friends, you'd be out all day long, and as long as you were home for supper, everything would be okay.

My grandfather must have been working at a gas station. That would have been the default. He didn't have the skills or the résumé for a white-collar life. Tom never graduated from high school. I'm not sure he'd even *made* it to high school—he told me he'd left school at the age of thirteen and joined the Merchant Marine. He didn't talk too much about his family, but from what I've been able to gather, he was treated horribly by his own mother. His dad left, and his mother would tell him, "I wish you'd never been born." So he had gotten to see a fair share of the world, gotten used to moving from place to place, going from job to job, always trying to get a leg up, always providing for Nona, and always providing for me.

Later on, when Tom got to be an old man, I had the chance to repay him, and I did. Tom was a proud guy. He didn't care about money. But when his last car was on its last legs, he called me and told me, "I'm gonna get me one of them Exploders."

That's what he called a Ford Explorer—an "exploder."

I said, "Okay, great. Why don't you go down to the dealer and look at one?"

"Oh, I'm not gonna spend *that* kind of money!"

Once, he came to our house and told Courtney, "You know, I don't need to live in a fancy neighborhood."

Courtney was taken aback. It was as if our home was a rebuke to him. She wondered if it hurt Tom's feelings, the thought that he hadn't been able to give me and Nona a fancier life. But I couldn't have loved him much more if he had raised me in a palace. Where would I have ended up if not for my grandparents? What would my version of the Merchant Marine have been?

Not that it matters, but I got that Exploder for him. He was driving his old car down from Idaho for a visit, and when he showed up, I had a brand-new Ford waiting for him in the driveway.

"Well, now," Tom said. "That's one hell of a vehicle."

"It sure is!"

"So you got one for yourself."

"No," I said. "It's yours."

I have a picture tattooed on my leg of me taking a picture with him, at the moment I gave him the keys. Grinning from ear to ear—he was so proud and loved that truck so much. He could tool around all day, he told me, and sleep in the back at night. I flashed back to my mother telling me, "Nona and Tom stole you from me." If I had believed her, I would have been stunned. But my mother could have just as easily told me that she'd been the first American woman in space. The truth is, she had a hard enough time just providing for herself and Ceci.

———

The next place we lived was Twin Falls, Idaho. We had a white house that was two stories tall, with a mudroom in the back and a coal furnace that went up the middle. One of my jobs was to go out in the mornings, grab the red wagon and two big buckets, and take them out to the coal shed. I shoveled enough coal to fill the buckets, dragged them back to the house, dumped them in the furnace, and started it. The whole house would start kicking, and then the heat would spread, spreading the smell of burning coal with it.

Nona and Tom had their bedroom upstairs. I slept in a bedroom downstairs, with a Jack-and-Jill bathroom that had another door leading out into the kitchen. Nona had a small radio there, and that was a magical thing. I became obsessed with a Jimmy Dean song called "Big Bad John"—a few years later, Steve Martin based "King Tut," the famous *Saturday Night Live* skit, on that song. I'd call the radio station and say, "Hi, I'm Frankie. Would you play 'Big John' by Jimmy Dean?" And a few minutes later, I'd get to hear the needle drop and then the song. That was the *definition* of magic. Who were these people I'd called? *Where* were they? Where did this strange music come from? How had it been made? And who had made it?

I'd call back right away and say, "Hello, it's Frankie. Could you play 'Big John' again, by Jimmy Dean?"

"Well, we can't play it right now. We just played it!"

But the next day I'd call back, and they'd play it again.

I'd been obsessed with a radio earlier too, when my mom and Ceci and I were living in Topanga Canyon.

That was a time when the three of us must have been flopping. Mom couldn't hold down a job, and sometimes that was her fault, and sometimes it wasn't: if she had a male boss, he was bound to start hitting on her sooner or later, and if her boss was a woman, there was a good chance that that boss saw my mom as a threat. She was still very young; she was still beautiful. She was uneducated, but she was well-spoken and charismatic, and she could still get any guy she wanted. I hate to say it, but this was before the #metoo era, and that was her real steady job: going from man to man. Some of those guys had nice homes, nice cars, and nice sound systems, like the one we'd had out in Hollywood.

But Topanga Canyon was different. Unlike any other place we had lived, there were other kids there. I wasn't upset, but I did find that strange, until I found out that those kids had a record player. It was one of those old record players where the needle was part of the lid, and you'd have to put the lid down to play it. I remember doing that with an Alvin and the Chipmunks single, and I loved that single so much that, for years and years, if anyone asked me what my favorite number was, I would just say, "Forty-five."

But one day I peeked down into the basement, where the older kids would hang out. There was a big antique console radio. It looked like a big jukebox or a TV with no screen, and it was turned around so that I could see the tubes glowing inside it. The older kid was fiddling around in there, and after a minute, the radio came on. The DJ was talking, and I thought, "Where is that voice coming from?"

That feeling's stayed with me over the years, right up to the point where I started doing radio myself. There was a storyteller inside that box, and I loved to listen to stories. If I didn't like where I was, a good story could sweep me away.

The house in Twin Falls had a basement too, crammed full of stuff that turned out to be fascinating. Old issues of *Time*. Old issues of *Life*. History magazines. Books with bindings that crumbled like dust when you touched them. The house was an old farmhouse that had been passed down from family to family for one hundred years, and this old, unfinished basement felt like the site of an archeological dig. In a way, I suppose it was.

There was another house, one hundred yards away from ours, and the people who lived in that house worked the farm we were on. We shared the coal shed, but their lawn was dirt and ours was nice and green. Nona and Tom didn't work on the farm, but somehow they had gotten the better side of the bargain.

In front of our house we had a corral. You could walk through it to get to the house, through a gate like the barbed-wire gate we had back in El Paso. You'd unhook the barbed-wire loop, come through, slip the loop back on its post, and walk down a pathway with sheep and sheep droppings everywhere. Candy was the name of the sheep I adopted. One day I came home from school, and she was laying on her side, dead and bloated up from the heat. That was a heavy thing—a heavy lesson about life and death, helping Tom bury her.

If you walked through a second wire gate, you'd be at our house. Through the back door, into the mudroom—there was a porch out in front, but we never sat on it. There always seemed to be too much to do. My grandmother had her clothesline out by the coal shed, and I had my BB gun, my slingshot, my fishing pole, and my dog, Barnaby—a black lab named after the 1970s TV detective Barnaby Jones.

Barnaby and I were always out hunting or fishing. Down a dirt road leading up from the house, there was a creek and a ditch that must have been fed by Snake River, because it had trout in it. With my gun, I'd shoot sparrows down from the trees. I'd hunt birds in the cornfields too. Then Tom gave me a .410 shotgun—the smallest-gauge shotgun you could get. That was a big deal to me at the age of thirteen. I had my dog, my shotgun, and we could hunt duck now and pheasant for Nona to cook. My grandmother would give me an old pillowcase and send me to get asparagus, which grew wild all the way out by the back of the farm. I'd ride my bike, I had my pocketknife, and I'd cut the asparagus down at the root, fill the pillowcase up, and my grandmother would make cream of asparagus soup—a favorite of mine to this day. She would make tons and freeze it. She was always cooking and canning, and we had freezers full of elk, venison, and birds Tom had hunted.

There weren't too many kids for me to play with—the houses where we lived were spaced far apart—but there were a few, and we'd go out to the railroad tracks that ran behind all the farms. We put pennies down on the track, and when we came back the next day, a train would have run over and flattened them. I'd get Tom's drill, make a little hole, put a piece of leather through, and wear the penny around my neck. But for the most part, I was happy being off by myself in my own secret places. Down where the cattle were on our land, there were big fields with pathways that led to large haystacks. I hollowed one out and put a blanket inside. That was my clubhouse, and I'd read the Sears catalog, look at the dirt bikes and motorcycles, and fantasize about riding them.

On the weekends, Tom and I went out bird hunting. Even when we were out fishing, we had our guns on us. If we saw a pheasant on the way down to the hole, we'd pull over, kill it, clean it, put it on ice, and bring it back with the fish. It was the same simple lesson I learned in Texas: you ate what you killed. And that was the problem with sparrows—I'd be out with my BB gun, shooting them, and Tom would say, "If you're not gonna eat them, you can't kill them." But I saw myself as a hunter. I was shooting all kinds of birds, lizards, and snakes. One day Tom was at work and Nona had gone into town, and I went into their bedroom and got Tom's 12-gauge shotgun, which he kept leaned up against a corner, loaded.

I took the gun out to one of the trees I'd hunt sparrows in, lifted it to my shoulder, looked down the barrel, leveled it, zeroed in on the middle of the tree, and pulled the trigger.

Voilà! Just like that, I had fifty birds, maybe more, lying dead at my feet.

I went back into the house, put the gun back in the corner it lived in, took all the birds, and started hanging them by their feet on Nona's clothesline. Knowing that you have to eat what you kill, I took the axe that we used to chop wood and started to chop their heads off and clean them.

When my grandmother returned with her shopping, there were feathers everywhere. Bird heads, bird guts, birds hanging down the whole length of the clothesline. I got into more trouble than I'd ever been in, and at that time, it didn't seem fair. Cleaning birds isn't so easy. First, you pluck the feathers. Then you open them a certain way and clean out the insides. Then you chop off the feet and the heads. A sparrow's so small, it takes doing—and I had tried to do the right thing. But come to find out, the reason that Nona had gotten upset wasn't just the wasted lives of all those tiny birds. That night, Nona told me that when she had first learned to drive, a pheasant had flown into the windshield, shattered the glass, and landed in her lap. Nona had been scared of birds ever since. And, of course, Tom had his own reasons for being angry: on top of everything else, I had taken his gun without permission.

These days, you'd never leave a loaded gun out and unlocked. But back then, we were taught about gun safety too. The first lesson being, don't touch someone's gun. That lesson was reaffirmed for me that day, in a way that made sure I would never forget it.

But the most memorable thing about Twin Falls—the best thing about our time there—was football. Even in New Mexico, long before I had met Carl and Alan, the Purple People Eaters, it was my favorite game. As a little kid, I played a lot of neighborhood football—a lot of flag football—and now I was finally old enough to join a real team. When I found out about tryouts, I couldn't believe it.

I was a fast kid and tough, and I felt comfortable out on the field. I made that team right away. Sometimes I played offensive tackle. But for the most part, I was a defensive end—number seventy-six. It felt amazing, spinning off the other team's offensive tackle, coming around the outside, and taking the quarterback out: pop in the ribs, hit him with everything, down on the ground, and he didn't get up.

I loved it so much. I was home. I was like, "*This* is what I'm meant to do."

Years later, my grandfather came to hear Mötley Crüe play. I had set myself on fire, and I was holding this mannequin up by a chain that came out of its head. Before the show, we had cut the mannequin's head off and filled the neck up with condoms, which we had filled with fake blood. When we played "A Piece of Your Action," our roadies would wheel the mannequin onto the stage. I'd pick it up with my left hand—with my right hand, I'd bang out an A—and Vince came out with a chainsaw, which got picked up by his microphone, and cut the mannequin's head off.

Blood sprayed all over me, all over Vince. In a small place, it was memorable. Afterward, Tom said to me, "You play rock and roll in the same exact way you played football."

That was spot on. Football gave me the same feeling I get when the band breaks into "Shout at the Devil." I play like an animal, and I have the scars to prove it. If you saw me up close, in person, you'd see right away: I'm as banged up as any old NFL veteran. I've had surgery on both my knees. Fractured my ankle. Had my hip replaced. I've got four bulging discs in my back, which I constantly have to stay on top of and will eventually have to have surgery for. Both my shoulders are a big mess—on my right side, they had to take muscles from my back and reconstruct the rotators, and that's something else I have to work on every day. I've torn my biceps, my hearing is damaged forever, and that's just a partial list.

The knees I damaged onstage, jumping off of stuff, blowing them out. The hip was repetitive motion. It turns out that I put my weight on my left side when I play. I lean hard into whatever I'm playing. I rock back. I rock forth.

The doctor told me, "You wore it down just like a guy on a factory floor after thirty years working with steel."

The shoulders I damaged by breaking guitars on the stage, Pete Townshend–style. We were getting ready to open up for the Stones, but a few weeks before the first show, I woke and could not move my right arm at all. It had been aching, and it had been weak, and I should have gone in to get it checked out, but this was way worse than what I had expected. Down at the hospital they said, "Sorry, bud. You've got to go in for surgery. Now."

I said, "No way. We're about to go out with the greatest rock band in the world. There's no way I'm going to miss it."

I convinced them.

"Okay, we'll give you cortisone to get you through. But as soon as you get a break, fly right back because once the rotators are torn, they snap back like rubber bands. Not only will they atrophy, but you'll also start to get scarification because you're not getting the blood flow you need."

I said, "Okay," and kept getting cortisone shots to deal with the pain. But being the rocket scientist I am, I immediately started breaking guitars with my *left* hand. So I now have two bad shoulders—and I'd torn my biceps off at the same time, just from the brute force of taking a piece of wood and smashing it, as hard as I could, into the floor.

Why didn't I loosen the screws? Cut the necks on those guitars? Mick and Keith could have told me: this thing that we do is show *business*—it isn't show *truth*.

But they didn't tell me, and I probably wouldn't have listened to them if they had. The one speed I had then was faster.

Now that I'm older and still don't want to be slower, I have to take much more care. Health and fitness, diet, and the amount of sleep I get, along with exercise—physical, but also mental—are real things to me now because there are real things I still want to do. When my kids want to go down the Snake River or hike up into the mountains, I want to be there. I want to keep up. Medication—that's not an option for me. But chronic pain's also a problem, and not only because it's a drag. Physical pain makes it hard to write poems, to write songs—to find the quiet place inside myself where that happens. It all starts to take tons of maintenance. You don't wake up anymore, look beautiful, and go out to run a marathon just because you can or because you might have something to prove. You wake up now, and you look like a train wreck, and you have to do yoga, stretch, and pray to God that you make it halfway down the track.

But I'm still the guy who sacks the quarterback so hard he doesn't get up. I'm going to make it *all the way* down the track.

Loyalty's super important to me. I learned that over the years, sometimes the hard way, when people I cared for and trusted were disloyal to me. But pride is just as important. Self-respect. Loyalty to myself. That's what I learned in Twin Falls, playing defensive tackle. I still remember my home uniform, green and white, on the hanger. I'd hang my pants up just so, hang my cleats off those, hang my shoulder pads over the top, and then my jersey, so that I could actually lug it back home—because Nona's role in all this was to make sure it all came back spotlessly clean. If you showed up in a dirty uniform, you did push-ups. So I'd take my uniform home every day, and the entire time—in halls, on the bus, walking through the field to the corral in front of our farmhouse—I'd be beaming with pride.

I was as proud of wearing that uniform as I was on the day I got my first bass.

And still, no one got that the black stripes under my eyes were a callback to my days playing football. No one, except probably my grandparents.

Jerome

Chapter 6

In those days, Jerome had a stoplight at the intersection of Main and Lincoln, which were the main streets in town.

That was the only stoplight in Jerome, Idaho.

Main Street cut through a park where the kids all hung out. Every once in a while, I'd go by on my bike. On the south side of the park, where the kids with the long hair hung out, I'd smell weed. I hadn't smelled that in the air since I'd lived with my mother. But there was only so much trouble for the cool kids to get into because Jerome was so small—everyone couldn't help but know everyone else's business—and half the people in town belonged to the Church of Latter-day Saints. Those Mormons were clean-living people, teetotalers. They didn't even drink coffee.

Nona and Tom were clean-living too, but they weren't church-goers.

Tom grouped preachers in with politicians. As far as he was concerned, they were all crooks, or enough of them were to spoil religion for everyone else. That set him apart, just a bit, in a town that was also full of Presbyterians, Methodists, Baptists, and Nazarenes. There were Catholics too, who came in for the summer. The migrant workers spoke Spanish and stayed in simple, one-story, two-family houses on the outskirts of town. In the fall, when the harvest was finished, they moved on.

Outside of those migrant workers, Jerome was the whitest place in the world. The most insular community you could imagine, with one new kid a year in the school at the most.

I had gotten used to being the new kid, but it still felt awkward. Everything did at that age. For the first time, I had started to feel uncomfortable inside my own skin. I was convinced I'd look better if I could just grow my hair long. But Tom wouldn't hear of it. If my grandparents had their way, I would have gone through life with a flat top. We had finally compromised on something that looked like a bowl cut, with bangs that went down to my eyebrows, but I was pretty sure it was a terrible look. Looking back now at my yearbook photo, I see I was right.

Then, to top it all off, I had just gotten glasses.

Today, I have glasses for reading, glasses for distance, and glasses to wear in case I lose my old glasses—which happens more often than it used to. But I especially hated those glasses, which had metal frames and made me look like I spent my time playing indoors.

The good news was that we moved to Jerome at the end of the school year. I had a few months to settle in before starting at school. Hopefully, I'd be playing football in the fall. In the meanwhile, I had the whole summer to look forward to.

Here in Wyoming, it would not be a good idea to jump someone's fence and go hunting. But in Idaho, in the seventies, it was not a big deal. Tom and I could just drive out of town, and if we saw ducks, quails, or pheasants, we'd pull over to the side of the road, jump the fence, and bag a couple of birds. We did that a lot over the summer and into the fall. We shot jackrabbits too, and in Jerome, you did not have to pay for potatoes. Potato farming was the big thing in those days—though dairy was on the rise and eventually took over—and farmers left the outside edges of their fields unplowed. You were welcome to dig for yourself and fill a bag to last you through the winter.

Tom was teaching me how to drive too, either in the El Camino or in Nona's orange Datsun 510. None of us knew it, but cars like that Datsun represented a turning point for the country. American muscle was on its way out. In 1973, the oil crisis was around the corner. It was the year of Watergate and *Roe v. Wade* and the year that the last American combat troops left Vietnam. The sixties were over, inflation was high, Nixon had just been reelected, and the steel crisis was starting—it was the beginning of the end of American manufacturing as everyone knew it. The slow end of a certain way of American blue-collar life. But 1973 was also the year of the New York Dolls' first album.

The New York Dolls are a huge band for me. Their clothes. Their attitude.

A lot of stuff shaped Mötley Crüe: Aerosmith's early albums, Cheap Trick, the Raspberries, Wings, Alice Cooper, and the Sex Pistols and the Ramones. But the New York Dolls were iconic— the flamboyance of their "fuck you." I modeled myself after Johnny Thunders, trying to split the difference between him and Mad Max. That's why I teased my hair out: I was trying my best to look like Thunders.

But I don't know if anyone outside of New York knew who Thunders was at the time.

It's a bit like that saying, "History is what gets written by the winners." In rock and roll, history gets written by the college boys. If all you read is *Pitchfork,* you might get the impression that all anyone listened to in the seventies were bands like Pere Ubu. Actually, everyone was listening to Pink Floyd, Bachman-Turner Overdrive, the Rolling Stones, Led Zeppelin, Black Sabbath, and Journey. They were listening to bands like Sweet, Slade, Deep Purple, and Free (I loved a lot of those bands), and hardly anyone was listening to Pere Ubu. No one in any place I'd ever lived had even *heard* of Pere Ubu. It took the world a long time to catch up, and now maybe no one remembers bands like Cactus and Uriah

Heep. But if you want to know what the seventies *really* sounded like, it's the sound of those bands, Steely Dan, and a whole lot of disco. When you look at the actual numbers, even the Sex Pistols had nowhere near the impact in real time that they had later on. (Except, maybe, in England, which is style crazy in ways that our larger, more lumbersome country is not.)

All that was happening, and all of it would shape and alter my life. But at the age of fourteen, I was completely oblivious. I liked the Datsun because it was easier to do donuts in than Tom's El Camino: rev the engine, dump the clutch, spin. I had a new bike too—a ten-speed with a working speedometer, which I thought was very cool.

But on some level, even way, way out in the sticks, I think I must have been aware that things were changing. I felt restless in ways I hadn't before. In Anthony, I had been too small to register the town's smallness. But I *knew* Jerome was small. It was idyllic. But something about it rubbed me the wrong way.

I wouldn't have been able to articulate it at the time—to Nona, Tom, or even myself—but I knew I had to get out.

A big part of that had to do with Uncle Don and with the records he'd started to send me. But some of it has to do with the fact that I'm an artist—and an artist is a little like somebody born with no skin. You feel everything. Then you grow up and make it your job to feel and interpret the world. Jackson Pollock did that by basically pissing all over his canvas. We did the same thing with mannequins, chainsaws, and condoms we'd filled with fake blood.

———

Uncle Don was married to Mom's sister Sharon. As a teenager, Don worked in his dad's record shop in Santa Cruz. One day a traveling record salesman asked him, "Have you ever thought about sales?"

Uncle Don hadn't, but that's what he ended up doing, for Capitol Records. Capitol had the Beatles. Capitol had the Beach Boys. Don rose quickly up the ranks, all the way up to vice president until, in the seventies, he became head of the label. But busy as Don must have been, he took the time to send me care packages: albums by Capitol artists like John Lennon, Paul McCartney and Wings, the Steve Miller Band, Bob Seger, Joe South, and Sweet. Sometimes Don sent cassettes. Sometimes he sent albums. Albums were better, because I could lose myself in the art and the liner notes, which I read—and reread, again and again—all the way down to the bottom.

This was what the bands looked like. This is what lyrics looked like, written out on the page. And it took producers to make an album, along with engineers, art directors, designers, photographers, typographers, tinters, and printers.

I loved to draw, I loved to write, and I had always been able to lose myself, for hours, in stories of my own making. Now my stories started to look more and more like song lyrics. It had never occurred to me to play an instrument. We never had a piano or a guitar in the house. So I didn't know what I'd do with those stories. I just knew that, for some reason, I felt a compulsion to write them.

I felt a compulsion to buy records too, because no matter how many Don sent, it was never enough. Records cost five or six bucks—Capitol records cost $5.98—and that was real money, back when the minimum wage was less than two bucks an hour. I'd go out and hunt for night crawlers, fill up carton after carton, and go door to door, all over our neighborhood, to sell them as bait. That's how I met Alan Weeks, who became my first friend in Jerome. Alan spent the summer of 1973 mowing lawns, and that's what he was doing when I met him. I was walking with my worms, and I waved; he waved back, and at that age bonds can form very quickly:

"Do you like the Eagles?"

"How could you not like the Eagles?"

Just like that, I'd made my first friend in Jerome.

We'd take our ten-speeds up to the park—that was the slow cruise, the circuit, and you were bound to see other kids along the way—and we'd go fishing down on Snake River. Back then, in Idaho, you could get a "provisional" driver's license at the age of fourteen. At fifteen, you could get a license with no restrictions. But if you were fourteen, you could take a car out. Technically, you needed to have an adult in the passenger seat, but no one in Jerome seemed to care. Every once in a while, Nona let us go out in the Datsun. We'd spin donuts down by the banks of the Snake, and one time we nearly spun off into the river. All the way home, I couldn't stop thinking about how I would have had to either tell Nona and Tom or pack a bag, hit the road, and disappear.

There was another time when we very narrowly avoided disaster. An older lady lived across the street from Alan's house. She had been widowed, and if she had ever had kids, they had grown up and left. But she had a big lawn where she'd let us play football. She gave us cookies. She was always nice, paying Alan to keep the grass cut and letting me dig in her yard for night crawlers. We went over there all the time, and late one evening—it had gotten to be dark already, but we were still playing catch—Alan's brother Darrin came out of the Weekses' house with a BB gun.

Alan had two younger brothers—Tracey and Darrin, who would have been around seven and eight. Tracey was out where we were, playing with his model car under the streetlight, and Darrin was barefoot, in shorts. He didn't have a shirt on, and the gun was stuffed in his waistband, cowboy style. For whatever reason, he decided to shoot out the streetlight.

He drew, and he nailed the light with the first shot. The kid would have made a great cowboy. There was glass everywhere. All of us started running. I ran right over Tracey's model car and smashed it, and the four of us tumbled into Alan's house. Scared to death that the cops would come catch us, we all hid in separate corners.

I don't think Alan's mom, Mrs. Weeks, would have lied to the cops. The Weekses were good, hardworking members of the Church of Latter-day Saints. Mr. Weeks worked at a gas station, like Tom. He sold night crawlers there by the carton, trying to make a quarter here, a quarter there. It was on the honor system, and Mr. Weeks's night crawlers always got stolen, probably by some of the neighborhood kids. (But never, in case you are wondering, by me.) He kept right on selling them, or trying to, because honesty was just the way he was wired. He was surprised every time he discovered that not everyone is wired the same honest way.

Well, we had just about calmed ourselves when the cops arrived. They knocked on the door. Mrs. Weeks answered. We heard her say, "Darrin and Tracey are sleeping. I don't know where Alan is, but he'd better be home for his curfew."

Actually, Darrin and Tracey were hiding in the bathroom. Mrs. Weeks didn't know that, and we never told her and never got caught. But I might have stayed away from Alan's house for a couple of days after that, because the next time I was over, all the broken glass had been swept away, and when I looked up, I saw the streetlight had been fixed.

———————

Jerome might have been small, but it had a downtown, with a JCPenney, a Western Auto, a Dairy Queen, and a couple of drugstores. Alan's grandmother worked at McCleary's, which had a real old-fashioned soda fountain with circular stools and a half-moon crescent counter. She lived above the store, worked as a cook in the back, baking pies, and Alan and I would go hang out and drink milkshakes.

McCleary's was a small-town drugstore straight out of the fifties. Most of whatever you needed, they stocked: clothes, tools, magazines, and dime-store novels. They even sold records. I bought a Pink Floyd tape, *Dark Side of the Moon*. Alan and I listened to "Money" over and over and over again on a battery-powered tape recorder we could take out of the house. I felt the bass line to that song at a visceral level. At around the same time, I heard Deep Purple for the first time—"Smoke on the Water" came over the airwaves one day on Nona's radio—and "Saturday in the Park" by Chicago. A few months after that, I was doing something in my room and Nona called out to me, "Hey, Frankie, that guy you like, Peter Cooper. He's on TV."

I knew what she meant. I didn't have any Alice Cooper albums, but I was interested *in* Alice Cooper, so I ran right out, down the hall and into the room where our TV set was. We had a little TV on one of the small TV stands you can roll across the room—and there, on *The Merv Griffin Show*, I got my first glimpse of Gene Simmons from Kiss.

Not Alice Cooper. But Simmons was interesting too. He was dressed up, full regalia, full makeup, big boots, devil horns coming up from his shoulders, just going for full-on shock.

Merv asked him, "Are you a *bat*?"

"Yes," Simmons snarled. "Actually, what I am is evil incarnate."
He leered at Merv's audience.

"And some of those cheeks and necks look really good," he said.
Then he hissed and stuck out his very long tongue.

It was silly, way over the top, and the guest sitting right next to
Simmons—an older comedian named Totie Fields—was rolling her
eyes and having none of it.

"Is your mother watching today?" she asked. "Wouldn't it be funny
if under all this, he was just a nice Jewish boy?"

You can see the exchange for yourself—it's on YouTube, and it
looks as ridiculous now as it must have back then. But then the full
band came out. They played "Firehouse," and even if "Firehouse" is a
rewrite of "All Right Now" by Free, it's still a good song. You really
can't argue with that chord progression.

It was a lot to take in. I didn't love Kiss's look. I didn't hate it.
I never became obsessed, the way some of my other friends did.
For other kids my age, Kiss became the seventies' equivalent of the
Power Rangers. They had Kiss lunch boxes and, later on, Kiss tattoos.
I paid more attention to their songwriting than anything else, and it's
funny: Once, we were co-headlining with Kiss, and I was playing our
song "Ten Seconds to Love." I was deep in the pocket, the crowd was
going wild, and suddenly I realized: "Whoa. I ripped this song off of
'Calling Doctor Love'!"

It was the same chord progression, and we were on the same tour,
and I hadn't realized how deep their influence on me had been. But
there I was, doing the same thing with Kiss that Kiss had done with
Free, without even realizing it.

Until Kiss and Alice Cooper came along, music had been getting
softer and softer. Jim Croce, James Taylor, Bread. I loved those lyrics
and the melodies. But the harder stuff I was starting to hear got me
going. I played it more and more loudly at home—and the volume
started to cause problems because our house was a double-wide trailer.

Watching Tom put the two trailers together had been fascinating. He made steps and poured concrete to make a driveway. He built a little work shed and put a fence around the backyard. I had a doghouse out back for Barnaby. Nona had a garden with fruits and vegetables she liked to grow. It was a nice place—the trailers were white and Nona always made sure they were immaculate, as was our yard. But it wasn't big. We had a kitchen, a front room, a little laundry room, and two bedrooms in the back, and the walls between those rooms were thin, so whenever I cranked my music up, Tom would start yelling: "Frankie! Turn that commie crap down!"

That's when I realized, "If I ever get a girlfriend, I'm not going to be able to do very much with her in here."

But when I finally *did* get a girlfriend, it wasn't like that anyway.

Her name was Susie. She had glasses with metal frames, like mine. A sweet smile too. Her dad called her "Sulky Sue" teasingly, but she wasn't sulky with me at all, maybe just a bit awkward. But, again, I was a bit shy and awkward myself—which was fine, because it seemed like we had all the time in the world to get to know one another.

We did that on walks, up to the Dairy Queen that stood on the end of Main Street and over to the ball fields just past it. It was like a Norman Rockwell painting come to life, literally Main Street, USA. Susie's mom drove the school bus. Her dad worked at the milk-bottling plant. I'd talk to Susie about Nona and Tom, about my sister Celia and how I missed her because she lived so far away. Sometimes we held hands, maybe kissed, and the whole world suddenly felt electric, woozy, and wild, even though, looking back, it seems very wholesome—and it was.

Susie's dad did not go to a church. "I worship God up on the mountain," he'd say. But Susie's mom attended the Nazarene church. Sometimes we'd go with her. There was a lot of singing of hymns, but I don't know that those hymns made an impression. What I mostly remember is shyness, mine and Susie's, as she sat on the bench beside me. Embarrassment at being seen in public with my "girlfriend." But also pride, because the girl I liked seemed to like me.

Jerome and Twin Falls both lie in the same Idaho valley—Magic Valley. Once a month, all the Nazarene churches in Magic Valley went to the roller rink in Twin Falls. Susie and I went together, even though I couldn't skate well and mostly held on to the wall. We went to the movies too, in Jerome's one movie theater—a single-screen cinema off Main Street, next door to the bank. We held hands. Sometimes we went bowling. And there was a record we listened to all the time: a Seals and Crofts song called "Diamond Girl." That became our summer song.

Twelve years later, when we were recording Mötley Crüe's third album, I tried to come up with an excellent cover. We tried "The Boys Are Back in Town" by Thin Lizzy—a great song, but we couldn't get it to work. We tried Elton John's "Saturday Night's Alright," but that didn't sound right to us either.

Then I said, "'Diamond Girl' by Seals and Crofts."

Everyone else in the band said, "You're crazy. This doesn't even sound like a rock song!"

We rehearsed it. The other guys were right—it wasn't going to work as a Mötley Crüe song. We covered "Smokin' in the Boys Room" by Brownsville Station instead, and that song, from the same year as "Diamond Girl" (1973), was Mötley's first top-forty hit. It went all the way to number three in the charts. But I sometimes wonder what would have happened if I had stuck to my guns and insisted on "Diamond Girl."

McLeary's Drugstore

Chapter 7

For a long time, it seemed like that summer would never end. Alan and I spent our time listening to music, riding our bikes around town, and drinking milkshakes down at McCleary's Drugstore. But ever so slowly, the colors started to change. By the time the migrant workers on the outskirts of town had moved on, school had started, and my friendships with Susie and Alan had started to cool.

I had won a few battles by then. Nona and Tom had finally allowed me to grow my hair out. It was down to my shoulders now, shaggy, and almost blond because I'd spent all of August rinsing it with lemon juice, sitting in the sun, and letting it bleach. I had a cool jacket too—a blue windbreaker with stripes. Best of all, I had a high school football uniform.

I was a freshman, but the way the town schools were split, with seventh, eighth, and ninth grade in junior high, and tenth, eleventh, and twelfth at the high school, freshmen—ninth graders—were kings of the hill at my school. So even though I was new in the town, I had a certain amount of status. I had long hair and a football jersey I could wear to class. More and more, I got the sense that the prettiest girls in class were paying attention to me. It wasn't so much that they *liked* me or acted like they liked me. But they didn't act like I didn't exist. The more attention they paid me, the less interested I became in Susie.

I'm not proud, looking back on it now. And I could have been nicer to Alan, who was crushed out then on the one cheerleader that every boy in our school was crushed out on.

Alan's big thing in those days was singing. He sang at his church, and his mother took him around to talent shows. The Mormons had their own circuit, and he'd sing "I'll Fly Away" or "Spread Your Tiny Wings." Sometimes he sang for little old ladies down at the local Moose Lodge. At school, he was in the chorus, and Jill, the cheerleader, was in chorus too.

One day she glanced at him, or he thought she did.

"Do you think Jill likes me?"

Alan wasn't a bad-looking kid. He had strong features, a jawline that implied real character—which Alan possessed. He was a serious, studious, sensitive boy, and he played football. But Alan didn't play football like me. He didn't seem to have the killer instinct.

"I don't know, Alan," I said.

I could have told him: Jill was out of his league. But Jill was out of my league too. She was out of *everyone's* league. She might as well have been a runway model in New York—she didn't belong in Jerome. But I didn't discourage Alan from asking her out. What I did instead was ask her myself, before he had a chance to. One day after school, I mustered the courage to go up and say, "Would you like to go see *The Exorcist*?"

Miraculously, she said yes.

I was elated. I was terrified. I spent two hours in front of the mirror, trying to get my hair to look right. Tom lent me the old truck he'd bought, and when I picked Jill up at her house, her smile was so wide and so bright, I even forgot my own fear. But for most of that drive, I was still as nervous as I'd ever been. The truck had a pleather bench seat, and I had fantasized about Jill sliding over—pictured my arm sliding over her shoulders. But Jill stayed on her side of the bench as I drove. I couldn't muster the courage to take her hand, and when the movie started, I didn't have the courage to kiss her.

What would there have been to lose? We had gone to Twin Falls because there was no way that *The Exorcist* would have made it to Jerome. It was way too transgressive, too frightening—and if Jill had liked me more, I'm sure that she would have ended up in my lap.

But I would not have known what to do if that had happened, and it didn't because, I am also sure, Jill had only gone out on that date out of pity, or some combination of pity and boredom—even if I had ditched the glasses by that point (I had finally convinced Nona and Tom that I didn't need to wear them all the time) and wasn't the worst-looking fifteen-year-old boy in Jerome.

Whatever the case was, we didn't talk too much on our way back home. We didn't stop by the Dairy Queen or McCleary's. We didn't kiss. And when I got to school on Monday, I didn't tell Alan about any of it. I felt guilty, but not for too long, because I was making new friends anyway.

Bubba, one of the few Mexican kids who lived in the town year-round, was the person I became closest to.

Bubba's name was Mike Garcia, but nobody called him anything other than "Bubba." He wore a windbreaker like mine, except his was purple. He was big: he wrestled, put the shot on our track team, and played on the freshman football team, which was divided, more or less evenly, between heavyweights and lightweights. Alan was a freshman lightweight, though he was a fast enough kid to play with the heavyweights, if speed was what was called for. I was skinny, so I switched back and forth too. But Bubba was as

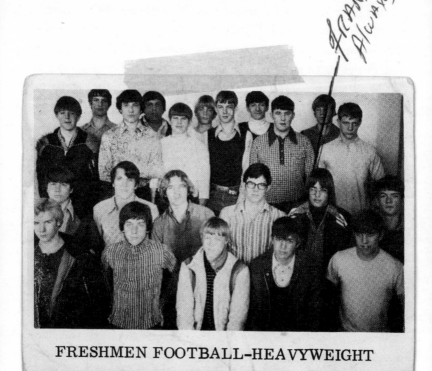

FRESHMEN FOOTBALL-HEAVYWEIGHT

big as any farmer's son—and Jerome had some real sturdy hogs on its team.

Every single one of us practiced hard, pushing big sleds and running wind sprints until we dropped from exhaustion. The school didn't bother with tryouts. If you wanted to play, you could play, and if you couldn't play, you got destroyed. Beaten up so badly that you wouldn't come back. Those of us who stayed played good ball. But regionally, we were too small to compete with the bigger cities. On an away game in Twin Falls, I played against some of the boys I'd known in middle school. Nona and Tom came down for that game, and I gave it my all because all of Twin Falls had come out for its team—everyone was screaming—and the Tigers had just a few families pulling

SCRAPBOOK

AUNT HARLENE, SHARON, MOM

WITH COUSINS & COOKER

ME

DAD - 1953

ME & JUAN IN EL PASO

WE ALWAYS HAD DOGS

NONA & TOM

ANOTHER BAD SCHOOL PHOTO

GONE FISHING

FAMILY REUNION: SHARON, NONA AND HARLENE

Mom.

SUSIE + ME

TOM, BOB, RAYLENE
+ ANOTHER BAD HAIRCUT

MOM WITH RAMON + HIS FAMILY (SEATTLE)

RICK AND LINDA / 1975

Linda ♡-

JOEL + KIM

ON MY WAY TO LOS ANGELE

JEROME, IDAHO — 1976

Over the summer, I'd been driving around with a much older kid. Hitching a ride, because I wanted to check out his very cool truck—a real hot rod from the fifties he'd had lowered. Over on Lincoln, he pulled the truck over to give a couple of migrant workers a ride. They hopped into the back, he cracked open a beer, and a couple of miles later, we pulled over to let those other kids out. As soon as they were gone, he let loose. He just unloaded on those migrant workers, calling them terrible things. I was shocked. All I could think about was Bubba—Bubba and his sweet old grandmother, who used to call me a hippie but welcomed me into her house.

Later on, I heard the kid with the truck had ended up in jail or in prison. But Bubba and I never saw or did anything that rose above the level of petty crime.

One day at McCleary's, I told him, "Stand there."

"What are you doing?"

"No, *there*."

"Why?"

"Bubba, don't worry about it."

On that day, I walked out of the drugstore with eight or nine records—my biggest haul by far. I didn't know what half of them were and could not have cared less. That was no longer the point. The thrill of stealing, and not getting caught, was the point. And Bubba was one of those people who'd listen to anything. To look at him, you wouldn't think that he liked Conway Twitty and Loretta Lynn. But he did. He liked their song "Rose Garden." He liked country and western and anything rootsy. He even liked jazz. I learned a lot from the way Bubba listened to music, and when I moved to LA and started working in record stores, I followed suit. I played ABBA as well as AC/DC. I'd go from Herbie Hancock to Generation X. I didn't *love* all of it, but I still learned from it. I learned it was good to see what other people had to say and all the ways they'd come up with to say it.

But that day at McCleary's, I didn't even stop to look and see what records I'd stolen. I just ducked in the alley and stashed them so that I could pick them up a short time later. Which I did. The next day, Bubba told me that a kid we both knew—the cleanest, most God-fearing kid, we both thought—had come up to him and told him, "I saw what you did. You and Frankie, you stole all those records, and I was going to go steal them from you. But by the time I got off work, they were gone."

So it turned out: even Mormons were down to do dirt.

Nona and Tom were not oblivious. But there was only so much my grandparents could do. I started sneaking out of my bedroom window and coming home at all hours of the night. After catching me two or three times, Tom took his nail gun and nailed the window shut. I found ways to sneak out all the same. In retrospect, I wonder if, by this point, I *did* want to get caught, because some of the stuff I did in Jerome seems unbelievably stupid. Once, out in a farmer's field, on older kid taught me how to huff gas from a tractor: stick a hose down, breathe the fumes in, and hold them in your lungs for as long as you can. When you let them out, you see birds, you see stars—you're just out of your mind.

It was unbelievably idiotic. But then I got a hose of my own. Walking down Main Street with Bubba, I'd stop and huff the gas out of parked cars. Bubba said, "Frankie, man. What are you doing? You're gonna get me in trouble!"

"Fuck it," I'd say. I was fearless. But the breaking point came when I took Bubba out to the toolshed Tom had built at the end of our driveway, and the two of us got incredibly high. It was so disrespectful of Tom and Nona. So lazy to not even bother to go down to the railroad tracks. I was asking for trouble and got it, because we got caught. Tom sent Bubba home. I got angry and went down to the tracks by myself to cool off. But later that evening, Nona, Tom, and I had a difficult talk—the upshot of which was that I got to go live with my sister and mom in Seattle, Washington.

Susie Maddox   Alan Weeks   Frank Feranna   Mike Garcia

Seattle

Chapter 8

Idaho was one state over—Jerome was one long day's drive away—but I may as well have landed on Mars. Seattle was a real city, full of record stores, music stores, thrift stores, and bookstores. It had an arena where all the top bands came to play. Amazingly, you could go see them for five or six bucks. I saw Led Zeppelin for the first time in Seattle: they had a sign with their name out on the stage. When they played their last song, "Black Dog," that sign burst into flames. It made a lasting impression. I saw Deep Purple, whose album *Burn* had just come out. Ritchie Blackmore, who played with Deep Purple, was my favorite guitarist. He smashed his guitar at the end of the show, roughing it up pretty good, bouncing it off the floor a few times, putting one leg up on the monitor, and breaking the instrument over his knee. It made for a slow, crunching, excellent sound and a brutal display.

I saw T. Rex at the Paramount Theatre, which is a palace today but was extremely grungy back then. The carpets were torn up, the seats were uncomfortable, the room smelled like piss. The Paramount had just one bouncer, named Tiny, but Tiny was seven feet tall and looked like André the Giant. Marc Bolan *was* tiny, and the audience got pretty wild, but Tiny could have held back the whole crowd by himself.

I saw Kiss at the Paramount too, opening for Savoy Brown. Midway through their set, Gene Simmons tripped over his cord and fell flat on his back. He kept playing, kicking his legs in the air like a beetle—the roadies had to rush out to get him on his feet— but the band was incredible. The volume alone was like nothing I'd heard. It was like standing too close to a Boeing, just something you felt in your chest. The adrenaline lasted for hours, and then I'd come home and my mom and I would go at it.

She had moved in with a man named Ramon, who worked at the University of Washington but was away all the time, setting up some sort of school in Mexico. Ramon taught at the state prison on McNeil Island too. So for the most part, it was Ceci, Mom, and me all over again, like it had been back in Los Angeles.

My sister was nine now and still stuck like glue to my side. What that meant, on a day-to-day basis, was that she would be caught in the middle when Mom and I argued—and my mom and I argued instinctively by this point. Only with hindsight can I say that I was angry and trending toward out of control, and my mom was aggrieved and probably guilt-stricken over not having raised me herself. At the time, it just felt like a god-awful mess. Invariably, I would tell Mom to piss off and leave home for hours—and, later on, days—at a time.

Because tenth grade had begun by that point, there were plenty of couches for me to crash out on. On the very first day of school, on the impressively large steps of Roosevelt High School, I met Linda, a striking girl with perfect dark hair that she parted on the left side so that the right fell in a curtain over one eye. It was a sexy look. Linda was very pretty, very shapely, and very outgoing, and we had struck up an interesting conversation when her boyfriend, Rick, walked up and reminded me (as he would several times in the weeks and months that followed) that she was also very taken. But by the end of that day, Rick Van Zandt had become my best friend in Seattle.

Rick was unusually tall—he stood two or three inches taller than me, and I had already grown past six feet. Rick had dark hair too, and it was unusually long. In those days, everyone had grown their hair out a bit: priests, politicians, TV news anchormen. But *truly* long hair, past the shoulders, either marked you as a hippie, still stuck in the sixties, or set you apart as someone ahead of your time. Roosevelt High School had all the cliques you'd expect a large high school to have—brains, jocks, greasers, and car jocks who spent all their time in the school's auto shop—but there couldn't have been more than ten guys who'd grown their hair past their shoulders.

Better yet, Rick played guitar. He was naturally gifted, and he had been playing since he was small. For a tenth grader, he played extremely well. He had a 1962 Fender Stratocaster, white like the guitar Jimi Hendrix had played at Woodstock, and an Ampeg V-4, which was the equivalent of a 100-watt Marshall stack. I got to hear it that very first day, because Rick's band played almost every day after school, and he made sure to invite me.

I was in my element. I felt like I'd found my people.

Mom and Ramon lived a couple of miles from the high school. I had to take two city buses to get to Twelfth Avenue, where Roosevelt was. But Rick lived a few minutes away, on Nineteenth. He had a huge, turn-of-the-century house that stood on top of a big, steep embankment. In the garage, there was a sliding aluminum door that went into a tunnel, which went underground and led into the basement. It was like going into Ali Baba's cave: a big, windowless room with chairs and couches, carpeting Rick had nailed up on the walls, and all of the band's equipment.

The band was called Oz—or maybe they had changed the name by that point to Pizazz, to make it more glam. The drummer, Sam Henriot, was the son of Zoaunne LeRoy, an actress. He'd just appeared in a made-for-TV movie with Sam Waterston and Tuesday Weld. *Reflections of Murder*, the movie was called, and Sam had been given a speaking role. He'd taken the money he earned and bought himself a massive double-kick drum set with a full rack of cymbals. It took up a lot of space in the basement and sounded as huge as it looked. The band's other guitarist, Joel Reeves, lived across the street. He played a Univox Les Paul knock-off and had an Ampeg V-4 like Rick's—both of them could hold their own, volume wise, even when Sam went all out on his drums. They had rigged up a bunch of lights too. Colored lights that they'd run through a foot switch, and at dramatic moments, they could flip the switch and flood the room.

With ten or twelve people down in that basement, it looked, felt, and sounded like a proper rock show.

There were a few things, however, that Oz lacked. They didn't have a singer and had to play instrumentals. That resulted in a certain amount of improvisation and soloing, but it wasn't too much of a problem because, in order to keep the audience interested, Rick and the guys glued the best bits of different songs into big medleys. They went from Alice Cooper, ZZ Top, Blue Öyster Cult, Queen, and Deep Purple to a bunch of Aerosmith's songs and maybe some Zeppelin before ending with their grand finale, "Rock Bottom" by UFO. They were good enough to make it work. But still, there was something else missing. I'd be standing there, studying them—paying more attention to Rick and Joel than I ever paid to my teachers—and I'd think, "They don't have a bassist. They *need* a bassist. If I had a bass, I'd be part of this band."

———

Ramon had an old, beat-up acoustic guitar with three strings. He never played it, and I never asked if I could, though Ramon and I tended to get along. Even when Mom and I fought—she'd send him to my room to straighten me out, but Ramon would just stand in the doorway. I'd be sitting on my mattress on the floor. I was always listening to music or writing in one of my notebooks, and instead of lecturing me, Ramon would ask about what I was writing or talk to me about his day. Sometimes he managed to coax me back out of my room. I was in love with music, and he had a hi-fi with big speakers. He was always playing Latin stuff out in the living room, Motown, Sly and the Family Stone. Mom would be smoking hash, dancing, and cooking menudo. I would think, "This is rad compared to boring old Idaho."

Sooner or later, though, things went sideways. With Ramon around, Mom was okay. With no man around, she seemed lost. She drank. She smoked three packs of cigarettes in a day. She just didn't know what to do with herself. After a drink or two, she seemed happy. She'd laugh. She'd kid around. But after three drinks, it would turn. She would get angry. She'd start to cry. Sometimes she'd lash out at Ramon. Mom could be sarcastic, she could be mean, and she was a good student of people. She wasn't stupid. She knew where to stick the knife in. She and Ramon would go out to dinner, they would go dancing, but at the end of the night, there'd be tears. My impression of Ramon was that he truly loved her and truly loved Ceci. He was a hardworking, disciplined man, and even though our mom pushed him away eventually, I know that he was a crucial part of Ceci's childhood. She still remembers him fondly. But I was older than Ceci. Ramon wasn't my father and didn't try to act as if he was. The two of us didn't fight like I fought with my mom.

Mom was always searching. Always reaching. Always desiring. Ramon was ambitious too, in his way—he must have been, with all the things he was building and doing. But unlike my mother, Ramon was at peace with himself. He was centered, and that allowed him to be more generous with those around him. One day after school, he knocked on the door to my room and gave me his beat-up guitar.

For that, I am forever grateful. That guitar was the first instrument I'd ever possessed. It turned my whole life upside down.

Teenage Wasteland

Chapter 9

Ramon showed me where to put my fingers: left hand on the fretboard, pluck the strings with my right. It wasn't that complicated. I didn't know what a chord was, but could I have played chords anyway with half the strings missing? All I needed to know at that point was to press down on a fret with my left hand and pluck.

There's a note.

Move to another fret, pluck.

That was a second note. Two notes together made a melody.

It was simple, but it wasn't boring. I was actually working the thing. I'd lose myself for long stretches, plucking out "Smoke on the Water," playing the same notes Ritchie Blackmore had played. But I got excited for real when I tried to read words I had written along with the music. Right away, the poems I'd been writing firmed up. They snapped into shape. I had always felt compelled to write notes and stories: if I'd seen a fight in the park, or driven past two crashed cars, or a jackknifed tractor trailer, I would have gone home, locked myself in my room, and written about it. But now I felt I would be able to *tell* my stories. Set to music they made much more sense and had five times the force.

I didn't know what I was doing. But it wasn't too different from what I did later with songs like "Primal Scream" or "Kickstart My Heart." The songs that I write are still simple: a few notes and some lyrics that tell a real story. "Primal Scream" is about my family. "Kickstart My Heart" was about an OD: "When I get high I get high on speed / Top fuel funny car's a drug for me." Those words alone killed the song as a single. Because of them, that song was never going to get played by radio stations back then. But "Kickstart My Heart" wasn't even a drug song. To me, it was a song of redemption, my way of saying, "Now that I'm sober, there are other ways to get high."

Seattle was where I realized that writing songs—trying to write songs—was a different kind of high. A better high in some ways. Longer lasting. One that still made me feel good the next day.

"You have hands," Rick told me after I'd been fooling with the guitar for a couple of weeks. We were at his house, and he'd let me pluck a few notes out on his Stratocaster.

"A lot of people, you try to show them how to play, and it doesn't feel right. But you look comfortable holding the thing."

Rick showed me a few tricks. "Don't put your fingers there. Do this. Slide between these two notes. See? That's a riff."

Sliding between two notes felt like something a bassist would do. But doing it didn't make me a real bassist. Being a bassist meant owning a bass, and to buy a bass I'd have to have some real money.

I'd go to Rick's house in the mornings and walk with him on his newspaper route. Along the way, I started checking parked cars to see if their doors had been locked. If they weren't, I'd open them, swipe the change out of change cups, and rifle through the glove box to see if there was anything else I could steal.

Before long, I had worked my way up to light breaking and entering, checking to see if front doors had been locked. The most that I got away with was a small stereo, stuffing it into the messenger bag that I had. Rick was a few houses down by that point. When he looked back and saw me, with half the stereo poking out of my bag, he glared at me like I was crazy. It was the end of that phase of my criminal career.

I was making more money in school, though. In the back of the school, I'd spread the *Diamond Dogs* gatefold out on my knees and roll joints for kids for a quarter a piece. I had fast fingers. I could get through ten or twelve in the few minutes it took for the next bell to ring. But no matter how fast I was, those quarters weren't going to add up to a bass.

Psychedelics were big at the time. Everyone in school started talking about LSD. First it was whispers; then all of a sudden the real thing was there, everywhere. Acid washed over the school like a wave. The batch we got ahold of was called Four-Way Windowpane. You were supposed to take one square and split it up into four pieces, but I had never seen acid before. I thought that one square was one hit, not four.

It was not a good experience. I wouldn't call it a bad trip, exactly. I'd say that it altered my mind. I don't think I've seen my hands, the clouds, a tree, the grass, or the mountains or heard my voice the same way again. I had always felt like a live wire: extremely awake and alert. When I was young, I saw it as passion, attributing it to my father and my Italian roots. Later on, I only saw the downside: all the times I'd been too sensitive. If you rubbed me the wrong way, the fire—the anger—came out. Today, I see it as a double-edged sword. I *am* passionate and sensitive. But I'm hypervigilant too: good at reading people, quick to read any room, very aware of my surroundings. In my line of work, it's a sort of superpower. But the problem is, you can't turn it off.

That's what that acid trip felt like. At first, it was great, like x-ray vision. Then you start seeing under the skin, to the flesh and the bones and the rot underneath. It's scary and doesn't shut off. But that didn't stop me from taking more acid. All it did, in the short term, was reinforce my belief that the things I was seeing and feeling deserved to be written down and sung about. It doubled my resolve to get ahold of a bass.

I came up with a plan. I had begun selling weed on the side. It felt like a natural progression from rolling, and if I prerolled individual joints instead of selling eighths and ounces, I could double my profit.

Then, through another drug dealer, I got ahold of a fair amount of mescaline. It came in the form of an off-white powder, like a lighter shade of cocoa. That gave me the idea of mixing it with cocoa and selling it at the school. "Chocolate Mescaline" was the brand name I came up with for this surefire thing. The entrepreneurial side of my personality was fully engaged. Rick and I bought some Contac cold medicine, which came in time-release capsules that we emptied out. Using a razor blade, we cut the mescaline with a packet of Hershey's hot cocoa mix and filled the capsules with chocolate mescaline. I planned to name my own price: mescaline wasn't so easy to get at our school. But my quality control wasn't what it might have been. Some of the kids I sold capsules to didn't feel anything. Others went mildly insane.

I never got busted. The other kids would have ratted me out, but before that could happen, the school kicked me out for a lesser infraction. I was in my usual spot, with the *Diamond Dogs* gatefold opened up in my lap, rolling joints. I was so intent on my work that I didn't notice the other kids scatter. I kept rolling, even after I felt the vice principal's hand on my shoulder.

I didn't even look up. I knew that I was in trouble. But I didn't think it was fair of the school to suspend me for *weeks*. Maybe they were glad to get rid of me. On my way home, I sat under the Twentieth Avenue bridge, smoked a joint, and told myself, "I'm not going back."

That night, my mother and I had the worst argument we'd ever had. The weed wasn't even my weed, I told her.

It was true! I had sold drugs, but I hadn't been busted for selling drugs. Plus, it wasn't like I was on drugs and she wasn't. She was. I knew, because I had stolen drugs from her. And I wasn't drinking a gallon of vodka a night either—it took me a few more years to build up to that point. All in all, I was still just an innocent kid. I was having sex now, and getting fucked up, but those were both recent developments. I wasn't drinking much. I wasn't smoking. Everyone smoked cigarettes, but I didn't.

This line of reasoning was lost on my mom. She must have known that I hadn't been doing well in school anyway. In class, my attention wandered. I was always doodling, thinking about music, writing little paragraphs, little quotes, little one-liners. But when I told my mother I wouldn't go back, she started to scream at me. I screamed back, Ceci started to cry, and I went to a friend's place—which is a part of the story the Mötley Crüe movie fudged but made a big deal of, so here's the truth: In the film, I take a knife and slice my arm open. When the cops come, I tell them my mother cut me.

In real life, I left the house, and as I was leaving, I threw a brick through the living room window. "See you later! Here's a gift on my way out."

My mom screamed down the street after me: she was calling the cops. I went to a friend's place, took a knife, and stuck it in my arm.

My friend said, "What the fuck? What's wrong with you?"

I said, "Just give me the phone."

It was then that I called the cops and told them that Mom had cut me with a knife. I saw it as a preemptive strike. But when the cops came—if they ever did come, to my friend's or my mom's—I wasn't around to talk to them.

I slept on the couch in Rick's basement. We didn't think that his parents would mind—they had six kids, so their house was already a madhouse. But when Rick's mother appeared at the top of the stairs to tell me that, actually, she did mind, I crossed the street and slept at Joel's. I slept at Sam's and at Linda's—her mother could have been running a home for wayward children for all the kids who would crash out there. I didn't go home, and when my two-week suspension was up, I still didn't see much of a reason to go back to Roosevelt High School.

I was having way too much fun by that point anyway.

Diamond Dogs

Chapter 10

I didn't start smoking until I was in my forties and going through a divorce. Before that, my band laughed at me: I'd take two puffs, cough, and put the thing out. During the divorce, cigarettes became a way of dealing with the anxiety without drinking. I smoked cigarettes for four years, and after I quit, I thought, "There's nothing left to quit, because I've quit it all." In my experience, it's mind over matter. You don't have to be that strong to quit anything. You have to *want* to. Withdrawal is painful, of course. But what you *have* to have is accountability to yourself. You *have* to keep your word. You can lie to other people but not to yourself. If you believe in a greater power, that doesn't hurt either.

I lived next door to Ravenna Park, just up from the University District, in a shared apartment in a four-story building. I slept on a mattress on the floor of the closet and put posters on the walls to make it cozy. Green Lake was nearby, and hiking trails connected Ravenna to Cowen Park, with a 7-Eleven at one end and a Stop N Go at the other. Both were open all night, and there was many a night that Rick and I stayed up until dawn, walking back and forth between the two.

Then I moved to an apartment where Joel's girlfriend, Kim, lived with a bunch of other kids who'd had to leave home for one reason or another. A two-bedroom in the University District, which is where all of us wanted to be anyway, walking around, rummaging in thrift stores. We had as many as ten kids crashing at any one time, but it didn't feel overly crowded because we were running all around town constantly—and when we *were* all there, it just felt like a party.

I started to hang with Rob Hemphill, who was the bassist in Roosevelt High School's other good rock band, Cold Daze. The two of us found long, cool scarves that made us feel like Keith Richards and Steven Tyler. We bought women's vests in those thrift stores, and women's suit jackets. We were so skinny, everything fit us. We'd take the clothes apart too, deconstruct them, and put them back together with weird stitching, pins, and armbands. It was the height of glam: *Diamond Dogs,* Mott the Hoople, T. Rex. Stuff that stayed with me well into the following decade. Many years later, when I was recording with Mötley, I thought back to "Future Legend," the opening track on *Diamond Dogs.* The first track on *Shout at the Devil* was my stab at swiping Bowie's intro. I called it "In the Beginning."

The books I was reading at the time stayed with me too. The University District had so many used bookstores. They're gone now, I'm sure. The University District itself has been torn up and rebuilt. It's not there anymore as I knew it. Roosevelt High School is gone—they kept the Roman facade but gutted and rebuilt the rest, so those grand steps are all that's left. But the bookstores are what I miss most, because they felt almost like second homes. I loved their musty smell. I'll still drop into a Barnes & Noble wherever I see one, even though Barnes & Noble smells nothing like that, and walk out with ten or twenty books.

In those days, I was drawn to the books behind the counter: the most frequently shoplifted books. They were the same books I would have stolen. I liked Burroughs, and I loved Bukowski. To this day, I reach for Bukowski whenever I write. I'll open one of his books and think, "Whoa, Nikki. You have to step it up now with your colors and your switchblade words."

The other thing I got from Bukowski was my love of muscular, eye-catching titles: *South of No North*, *Tales of Ordinary Madness*, *Notes of a Dirty Old Man*, "Two Kinds of Hell." Titles that stuck in my mind like shards of glass. As a songwriter, I've done my best to measure up: "Too Fast for Love," "Dr. Feelgood," "Kickstart My Heart." Those are eye-catchers too. Anthems. *Theatre of Pain* I got from Artaud, the surrealist writer, and his Theatre of Cruelty—a variation on the theme.

There's nothing like a good anthem. I was in my twenties when I wrote "Shout at the Devil," but "Shout at the Devil" unified a bunch of teenagers. It made them feel empowered. It made them want to rebel. They were coming into their own emotionally, intellectually, physically, sexually, and I wanted to give them something to say: "I don't like Mom and Dad's music! Mom dresses stupid, and Dad is a putz, and this is our battle cry: 'Shout at the Devil'!"

That's what T. Rex, Aerosmith, and *Diamond Dogs* had done for me already. It's what Burroughs and Bukowski were doing for me at the time.

But I had to work to pay rent, to buy books, to buy clothes, to buy all the records I wanted to listen to until the grooves wore down. I was a dishwasher at a Greek restaurant. I was a dishwasher at Victoria Station. Then I got bumped up to the salad bar. That job gave me a vantage point. What I saw was that half the people we served never finished their food. I'd take a knife and cut the uneaten ends off their steaks, run the meat through a meat grinder, and stash the results in a five-gallon bucket. Then I'd take the bus back to the University District, and everyone in the apartment would eat. Sometimes we ate hamburgers morning, noon, and night, watching *Don Kirshner's Rock Concert*, hoping that the Raspberries or the New York Dolls would come on, with hamburger grease and the stink from that meat bucket wafting through the air all around us.

Rick spent a lot of time in that apartment, and I spent a lot of my time at his house, listening to his band play.

I spent just as much time with Rob Hemphill. The guys in his band were a cut above my friends. At least, they carried themselves in that way. It was an interesting time over at Roosevelt High School. Busing was a new thing in those days, so the building had recently been integrated, but it was still segregated in many respects. Kids from well-to-do neighborhoods like Laurelhurst and Sand Point went to the school, and there were real class distinctions. Guys like Rob Hemphill, from rich neighborhoods, walked around in leather jackets. Guys like Rick and Joel couldn't afford leather jackets. Rob, nevertheless, respected the fact that Rick and Joel were musicians. He came by and jammed. But his friends might have looked down on us. They probably saw us as the quasi-hippie, heavy metal kids that we were. They smoked hash, we smoked ragweed, and they thumbed their noses. Cold Daze had smaller amplifiers than Pizazz. They weren't as loud. But they had a PA system, and that made them a more complete band than Pizazz. It meant they could have vocals, and as a result, they were much more popular. They were high school bands at the same school, so as rivalries go, it was friendly. But beneath it all, there was real tension.

If I moved freely between these factions, it was because I had gone, very quickly, from being a new kid in the school to not being in the school at all. Rob moved freely because even among the rich kids, he was seen as well-off. His parents owned Hemphill Oil. They had their own fleet of heating oil trucks. That kind of money made Rob a sort of aristocrat in our world. Rob was a year older. His hair was almost as long as ours. In the school's more highfalutin circles, having long hair was one more thing to look down on. I can't imagine what Rob's friends said about us when we weren't around, but no one dared criticize Rob.

As for me, I had just dyed my hair silver. It was something I'd seen on a poster: Mott the Hoople's bassist, Pete Watts, had a great big shock of silver hair.

"How did he do that?" I said to myself.

The answer I came up with wasn't dye. It was spray paint. It was a perfect solution, because the paint basically turned all my hair into straw. It made my hair stiff—I could manipulate it and make it look as crazy as my imagination could get. Rob thought it was cool in a genuine way. But that's how Rob was: cool in a genuine way. He didn't give much of a damn. He wasn't self-conscious. He wasn't repressed. He liked to have a good time, and that drew us together. He acted as if he had nothing to lose, whereas I really didn't have all that much to lose. And the other thing we had in common was our interest in bass guitar.

Rob played a Gibson—a Les Paul Recording Bass, which is shaped just like a Les Paul guitar. It's not an instrument you see all that often, but it made an impression on me. (Later on, I came to own one. It looked much better than it sounded.) I was desperate by now to have a bass of my own. I'd go down to Broberg's music store on University Avenue and peer through the window.

A good bass was not cheap. Even a not-so-good bass was outside of the price range of someone who'd barely been bumped up from minimum wage. I hadn't even been able to keep up with rent and was crashing with a girl I had been dating. But I made up my mind: I needed a bass, and I was going to get one. After practice one day, I asked Joel, "Can I borrow your guitar case?"

"What for?"

I wouldn't tell him. I just said, "I'll be real careful. I'll get it back to you tonight."

I was careful, and he did get his case back—after I took it down to Broberg's.

I walked in and struck up a conversation with the man behind the counter. "I'm a guitarist. I'm new in town, and I need a good job."

We chatted for a bit, talking about bands that both of us liked. After a while, the clerk said, "Hold on, let me get you an application."

As soon as he went into the back of the store, I took a Gibson off the wall and shoved it in Joel's empty case. I did it so quickly, I had time to collect myself before the man came back out. Using a fake name and a fake address, I filled out the application. Then I shook the man's hand and, calmly as I could, walked out of the store.

That night, we gathered at Rick's place. I was beaming with pride, but I wouldn't tell anyone what I had done until the whole gang was down in the basement.

Finally, I opened the case.

"Check out my new bass," I said.

None of the other guys smiled. They just looked at me mutely.

"Frank," Rick said. "That's not a bass."

I looked down at the Les Paul—a beautiful gold top.

"Count the strings," Joel said. "It's a guitar."

They were right, but there was nothing I could do about it. No way to return a stolen guitar.

I should have held on to it. A 1974/1975 gold top Les Paul is a beautiful thing. But I sold it right away to a couple of brothers who played in a band across town—the Telepaths, they were called. The brothers were punks, or whatever "punks" were in that thin slice of time between the Dolls and the Ramones' first album. Gnarly dudes I sometimes hung out with, but I got a good-enough price—enough to get an actual bass, which I did at a music store that wasn't the one I had robbed. I got a black Rickenbacker, which wasn't quite as cool as Rob Hemphill's axe but was still a formidable thing that I eventually traded in for a Fender. But a few days after getting that bass, I was talking to Rob's guitarist—a talented guy who remains nameless here because I tracked him down recently (he's a real estate agent), and he denied that any of this ever happened. But it actually *did* happen. It happened exactly like this:

"A gold top?" the guitarist said. "Hell yes, I'll buy it off you."

That night, I went back to the brothers' place. They lived with their parents, and I had to wait until all the lights in the house had gone off. Then I snuck in through a window, went down to the basement where the Telepaths rehearsed, and snuck out the back door with the Les Paul. The next day, I sold it to the real estate agent in training. But that's not the end of the story, because the night after that, the Telepaths came looking for me.

My girlfriend lived with her parents, so she had her bedroom upstairs, and I had a small room in the basement. The whole setup was a bit weird because the girl's parents had been separated—they may have even gotten divorced—but neither one had the money to move. They had their own bedrooms too, and they both worked two jobs and had a daughter who was kind of, sort of going to school and another crazy teenager down in the basement, trying to learn to play "S.O.S." by Aerosmith on his bass—which is what I was doing when the doorbell rang.

The brothers were pissed. They both had scissors, which they were holding like knives.

"We're going to cut your hair, dude," one said.

The other one just said, "You stole our guitar."

I fought like a rabid dog. I had a nice black eye and a split lip, but they never got to my hair. I wasn't long for Seattle after that. But it was a Rolling Stones concert that put it all over the edge.

The Stones were playing the arena, naturally. The price was outrageous: ten bucks. There was no way any of us would have paid that, even if the show hadn't sold out (which it had). But we loved the Stones, and Rick and I and a bunch of other kids went down to hear what we could hear from outside the coliseum. It was a scene: half the city had the same idea. My friends and I sat down in a circle. Someone had weed, and I offered to roll it. But the thirty seconds it took me to roll a joint in those days was also the time that it took for a cop on a horse to ride up and arrest me.

It happened so quickly, my head was still spinning a few hours later.

"We were all like, what the hell happened?" Rick said the next time I saw him.

"It wasn't even your weed!" said Joel.

But in the few days since I'd seen them, I had made up my mind once again.

It was time to say goodbye to Seattle.

Back on the Farm

Chapter 11

I took a Greyhound bus back to Jerome. I had my Fender bass with me, a duffel bag full of clothes, some cassettes: T. Rex, Aerosmith, and Bowie albums. My grandparents drove down to meet me. When she saw me standing there, Nona couldn't stop herself from saying, "Frankie, what happened?"

I was wearing platform boots and an old women's jacket I'd turned inside out at some point and resewn. My hair was spray-painted silver. But Nona and Tom took me back. They accepted me. I got a job laying pipe, literally, on John McGonigal's farm. It was what Bubba was doing, and I hated it. The mud was eight inches deep. I made it half a mile down the line before I sat down, crossed my legs, and told Bubba, "Fuck this."

Dishwashing had not been so fun. The hours would turn into taffy, and each shift seemed to go on for days. Irrigation was like that but worse—a lot worse, with the sun beating down on your head. But there was nothing to do the next day but go back. Bubba had laid the rest of my pipe that first day, and it had all but killed him. He let me know that he wasn't about to do the same thing again.

I started having trouble with other Mexican kids who worked on the farm. I had had to fight in the hallways of Roosevelt High

School—kids who got bused in pushed me up against walls, tried shoving me into lockers, called me "Alice Bowie" and "faggot." I had to stick up for myself. In that sense, the fields were nothing new—except that now I had a pipe to defend myself with. Later on, in the clubs in Los Angeles, fighting became a sport, not a burden: the same thing that had intimidated me in high school, I came to embrace. But I wasn't in LA yet, and being called names, teased, taunted, and sucker punched wasn't much fun.

On the other hand, Bubba had my back, and that pipe did a lot of work for both of us. Irrigation paid better than dishwashing did. And I needed the money because I had my eye on another guitar.

Whenever Tom and I had gone to Twin Falls, we'd stopped by a place called Red's Trading Post. Red's was a gun shop, and Tom was always looking at guns and rifles to take hunting. But you could pawn stuff there too, and someone in Twin Falls had pawned a Univox guitar. It was a Les Paul copy, similar to the Vox that Joel Reeves played in Pizazz, with a beautiful sunburst finish.

In Seattle, I had put in some time with the guitar player in Cold Daze. We'd sit on the back steps of the school, and he'd show me tricks—like Rick, he was a gifted musician—and, of course, Rick had shown me a bunch of stuff too. I preferred the bass, and still do, but I could bang out a few basic chords, and it's always a good idea to have a guitar around. Today I have them all over the house. I never became a good guitarist. If I spent six months playing for two hours a day, I'd get good enough to join a band. If I'm rusty, you probably don't want to listen to me. But there's stuff that I've written on bass, and stuff that lends itself more neatly to a guitar. "Don't Go Away Mad"—that was a guitar song. I wrote "Shout at the Devil" on an acoustic guitar, playing as hard as I could to get maximum volume. "Knock 'Em Dead, Kid," "Red Hot," "Ten Seconds to Love," and "Kickstart My Heart" all started out as acoustic guitar songs, and I should have walked out of Red's with an acoustic—I would have gotten more use out of it. In Jerome, I didn't even have an amplifier.

But something kept drawing me back to Les Pauls, and even without an amplifier, the Univox made some noise if you played with a thick pick and banged away hard.

I carried that guitar around town. That was another reason to have gotten an acoustic: a Les Paul isn't light, like a Fender. But I carried mine everywhere. When I'd been in Jerome for a couple of months, Uncle Don and Sharon came up from Los Angeles to visit Nona and Tom. Their boy, Rick, was still a small kid. But their daughter, Michele, was just a few years younger than me. I invited her down to the park. I brought the Les Paul and banged away for an hour as we sat on one of the benches.

"I'm going to be a rock star," I said.

It didn't occur to me that Michele had probably met actual rock stars. To me, the idea that rock stars were real people was still pretty foreign. I thought of Rick Van Zandt as a rock star. Rob Hemphill was a rock star, but Peter Frampton, Marc Bolan, and Bowie were more like gods. More like stars in the sky: "Look! There's the constellation

Deep Purple! Over there, following the line up from Ritchie Black-more's guitar, you'll see Uriah Heep!" That's how far away and abstract it all seemed. But after dinner, Don pulled me aside and said, "Frankie, our home is your home, and we will always welcome you."

That felt a lot less abstract.

SCRAPBOOK

NOTHING TO LOSE

THE WHEREHOUSE
records • tapes • records

FRANK

ALWAYS READING   ALWAYS WORKING

ALWAYS WRITING

SHARON & DON'S

CH-CH-CH-CH-CHANGES

WITH ANGIE, 1978

BLACK HAIR, DON'T CARE.

JOHN ST. JOHN, ME
+ LIZZIE

DANE

LIZZIE

ANYTHING TO GET NOTICED

ABOUT TO TAKE

OVER THE WORLD

TAKE ME TO THE TOP

LOS ANGELES, 1980

Bob and Harlene drove their motor home up for a visit. They were living in Palm Springs now, but on their way home, they were going to drive through Los Angeles, where their daughter Raylene had an audition. Raylene wanted to be an actress. She was a tiny thing then, but apparently she had real skills, because she had gotten an agent and was trying out for a part in a western. They didn't need to ask me twice if I wanted to come along for the ride. I had just gotten off work for the day, I had mud up to my ass when I saw them, and I didn't even want to take the time to shower. I wanted out of Jerome right away. As soon as I saw them, I said, "I'm quitting. I want to go to Los Angeles."

It's a strange thing, but Nona and Tom kept my bedroom like it was on the day that I left, all the way through to the day of my grandmother's death, after which Tom sold the double-wide trailer.

In those days, you could go into a record store and ask the clerks if they had any promotional posters they were about to throw out. Sometimes you'd even get a cutout of the band. So I had the poster for *Frampton Comes Alive!*, an Aerosmith poster, a Uriah Heep poster. I had Sweet posters that Uncle Don had sent up from Los Angeles. And you could get cutouts at music stores too: life-size cardboard facsimiles of musical instruments. I'd taken a cutout of a Les Paul bass and hung it, upside down, on the wall—and a lot of these things were still there years later. When Mötley Crüe was getting ready to release *Theatre of Pain*—the album with "Home Sweet Home" on it—I drove up from Los Angeles to see Nona and Tom. It wasn't the best time for me, and I had become nostalgic for my grandparents. The way Nona and Tom both had cups of coffee in front of them at all times. The brown More cigarettes that Nona smoked. All the nights we had spent playing cards and Yahtzee. So I came home and slept in my old room, surrounded by all my old stuff. It was profoundly moving to realize that, even though I'd never lived with Nona and Tom again after leaving with Bob and Harlene, they had kept this safe, welcoming space warm for me.

It was as though I had never left.

But I did. When Bob and Harlene left for California, I left with them.

We had gotten as far as Bishop, California—not too far across the state line from Nevada—when Harlene checked in with the agent and found that Raylene had missed the audition. I don't know if my aunt and uncle had screwed up the dates or if the producers had decided to cast someone else or simply decided to go in another direction. But they were no longer in a rush and decided to take the time to see Yosemite, which was nearby. They asked if I wanted to come. But I couldn't get to LA fast enough. So once again, it was me and my bass—Nona and Tom had promised to send my guitar down, along with some of my posters. I had my bag full of clothes and some tapes. I got on a Greyhound again. But this time the bus was bound for Los Angeles.

Sharon met me there, at Hollywood and Vine, at the very same bus stop Marilyn Monroe dreams about in the film *Bus Stop*. The Capitol Records building—a white tower that's circular, like a stack of 45s, and one of the most beautiful structures on the West Coast—was half a block away. My uncle Don was in charge of the whole operation.

It was everything I'd dreamed about, ever since Don started sending those records to me in Jerome.

I was eighteen years old. By the time I turned nineteen, I told myself, I would be signed to Don's record label.

––––––––––

Don and Sharon lived in Northridge when I moved in with them, in a three-garage, four-bedroom house at the end of a quiet, tree-lined cul-de-sac. I was in awe of the place. The first thing I noticed when I walked in was the beautiful tile in the hallway. The colors were so deep and rich and luxurious. I had never been in a home that was nearly as nice. It wasn't *too* big. It wasn't palatial. You might have expected the president of Capitol Records to live in a mansion. But compared to Nona and Tom's double-wide, it felt incredibly posh. There was a small swimming pool, a side yard, a patio with a picnic table. Outside of that tiled entryway, the whole house had shag carpeting—green shag that Rick was always dousing with alcohol and lighting on fire. Michele was a sweetheart—just a wholesome Mormon girl. She was into square dancing and playing the piano, and she loved to sew. She was fantastic. But I kept an eye on her brother. I imagined him setting my hair on fire when I slept and kept my bedroom door locked in case he ever had the idea.

Don and Sharon were Jack Mormons, which meant they smoked and drank wine. Don had a bar—he and Sharon loved to entertain— and they stocked it with every imaginable kind of liquor. The bar had a polished top, with 45-rpm records Don had had lacquered over. There were a few pachinko machines in the house too, and Don had a fifteen- or twenty-foot wall of LPs. Thousands upon thousands of records.

I was in heaven, but before I could even get used to this setup, Don and Sharon moved us to a place that was quite a bit nicer.

We were in La Cañada now—"The Canyon," north of Los Angeles proper—in a sprawling, single-story ranch house that had been built by a large LDS family. The home had twelve tiny eight-by-eight bedrooms, and Don took three or four of those rooms, knocked the walls down, and made us a huge music room. He put his record bar there, along with Michele's piano. We had wall-to-wall carpeting—white shag—that Rick immediately started lighting on fire. We had a big, modern kitchen and a beautiful dining room. Every night, we ate dinner together.

Nona was always a great cook. My mother was a great cook. And Sharon also turned out to be a wonderful cook. Sitting down to dinner as part of this large, comfortable family was a wondrous thing.

It was very green where we lived, very rural, with horse trails running behind the house; the San Gabriel Mountains rising above us; and coyotes, skunks, possums—even the occasional bobcat—making their presence known. In our backyard, we had a large pool, a tennis court, and a little guesthouse. I can picture the kids jumping in and out of the pool, eating hot dogs and drinking lemonade, and Uncle Don sitting shirtless in a lounge chair by the pool. He had the first tattoo I recall seeing—one he'd gotten in the military. Aunt Sharon looked a bit like my mother, with big blue eyes that were bright, like a candle was burning behind them. She was an immaculate dresser—I don't think I ever saw her without makeup on. I've seen 8 mm film of her smoking, but I never saw her smoking in real life. She may have been a bit reserved, a bit aloof with new people. But with us, she was warm, very loving—she didn't have my mother's biting, sarcastic streak. There was nothing intimidating about Aunt Sharon, and I loved her. But I looked up to Uncle Don. Don was educated in a way that the rest of my family was not. Nona and Tom didn't have passports. They had never been to New York. But Don had traveled all over the country, and he'd seen a fair share of the world. He had black hair, a big laugh, and a big smile. He exuded confidence. He was the president, after all, and I was a bit in awe of him and maybe embarrassed by all the new things he tried introducing me to—not because I didn't like them but because I was ashamed not to have known all about them already.

The Olympics, for instance. I was sitting in our armchair with Don's gigantic headphones over my ears, blasting *Alice Cooper Goes to Hell*, when Don came out and said, "Frankie, do you want to watch the Olympics?"

"What's that?" I said. I honestly didn't know. I knew what football was, and in La Cañada, I had played tennis for the first time. But that was a sign of how provincial I was in those days: the Olympics just wasn't a thing that had ever come up. In some ways, it made me feel like an outsider. What *I* knew was Alice Cooper. So I worried sometimes about not knowing how to fit in with this perfect family. But then I'd say something to make Uncle Don chuckle, or Sharon would come along and say something comforting, or Michele would ask me for help with something she was working on in the crafts room where she did all her sewing, and I would remember that, no, I was family, and it was okay for me to have nice things and a solid roof over my head. It was a long way from where I'd been six months earlier, sitting in Bubba's basement, listening to the Edgar Winter Group, looking at girlie magazines. It was still a bit jarring, but I had it good.

Don took me under his wing in other ways too. He helped me get a job, down at a Music Plus record store in Glendale, and let me drive his F-150 pickup to work. Don's truck had fat tires in the back, it had cool rims, and the front was a little bit lowered. I thought I was the bee's knees, driving around in that thing, blasting music, going to the mall. Sometimes, on my way to work, I would pick up my boss, the record store's manager. The guy was probably twenty-three or twenty-four, but to me he felt like a fully grown authority figure. He had long black hair and was missing one of his arms, which was fascinating to me, and he'd be listening to Miles Davis or some German rock band. Sometimes we'd smoke a joint before leaving, and he'd turn me on to things I'd never heard: Devo. The Ramones' first album. Stuff that was faster, spikier than what I was used to. At work I'd play ABBA and AC/DC albums back-to-back. I'd put on the Raspberries and Eric Carmen's solo stuff and marvel at how lush and ripe those songs were: "No Hard Feelings," "Never Fall in Love Again," "All by Myself" (long before Celine Dion covered it).

Years later, I found out that Carmen was ripping off Rachmaninoff. It made perfect sense: the strong classical influence. But in music, everyone steals from someone.

———

I was stealing too, from Cheap Trick in the daytime, when I practiced and practiced and tried to write my own songs, and from the record store most every night. Sometimes, if an especially good record came in, I would set it aside and sneak out with it later. More often, I padded the till and went home with an extra ten or twenty dollars.

I had my bass. I had my guitar. I did not have an amp to play them through. So I stole until I had stolen enough to buy one that was as loud as the amps Rick and Joel had had up in Seattle. Now I had the equivalent of a Marshall half stack in my room. I had posters I'd brought home from the store and a few that I had asked Nona and Tom to send from Seattle. I had a girlfriend named Katie who I'd met down at the store, and I'd sneak her into the guesthouse. But Don and Sharon were not idiots. They saw me high sometimes, and once I had gotten that amp, the whole neighborhood heard me playing guitar. I'd talk to Uncle Don about my plans to be a musician, and now that I'm older than he was then, I can guess what he was thinking: "Frankie, dude. You're so loud. And you do have this dream. But nobody makes it in this business. Trust me, I know. Musicians come and go. They have a hit, or they don't have a hit. Either way, they end up working at 7-Eleven. *I'm* the only guy who's making money."

I've had that talk with my own kids. I tell them that they can do anything they set their minds to. I tell them, whatever it is, I'll support them. But no matter what, they have to have a business plan. They need to take courses. They need to be smart financially. I didn't have any of that. I didn't graduate high school. I was trying to play heavy metal, smoking dope, working in a record store. Don would come home from the office and hear my guitar from a half mile away. I'm sure that he and Sharon had a few late-night talks: "I'm worried about Frankie. He's got no schooling. There's no backup plan."

They would have been right. There was no backup plan. I was a long ways away from the Stadium Tour—and, as Bon Scott once observed, "It's a long way to the top if you wanna rock 'n' roll."

But I was closer than I had been in Seattle or in Idaho, and when Don and Sharon finally got fed up with the pot, the noise, and the example I was setting for little Ricky—who was shaping up to be more of a criminal at his age than I'd ever been—it wasn't the worst thing, because even when they kicked me out, they made sure I knew that they loved me and that I would not be alone.

Eruption

Chapter 13

Don helped me get a one-bedroom in Glendale and cosigned the lease. Sometimes I lived there by myself. Sometimes I'd have a few roommates. Sometimes I'd have more than a few, sleeping on mattresses on the floor. I had an old Buick—a real rust bucket from 1948—that I'd paid a hundred bucks for. I had to pump the brakes over and over and over again to make it come to a stop. That's when I learned about air in the brake lines and figured out how to change brake pads. I didn't have the money for a mechanic.

I'd take the Buick to Burbank, where my new job was. I'd been fired by this point for stealing from the record store. Now I was cleaning rugs, carpets, and furniture. The steam cleaner was just a big box with a hose—you poured water in, it would heat, and you steamed carpets and furniture clean. Every day I picked it up in Burbank and went out on house calls. I figured out very quickly that I could wedge the big machine up against a door and leave it running while I rifled through medicine cabinets. I'd steal some pills, split a few with my friends, sell the rest, and buy musical equipment: pedals, effects boxes, cords. But I lost the job because of Scotchgard—an upsell the company used. I'd tell the customer, "I'll do your whole house. It costs $120, but I'm putting myself through college. If you help me out, I'll do the whole house for $50."

I used plain old water instead of Scotchgard. When I brought the steam cleaner back, I'd tell my boss, "Sorry, no one went for the upsell today."

Then I got called out to a house in Topanga. The owners were hippies, they had tons of cats, and the cats had pissed all over one of the rooms.

I checked it out and said, "Okay. We have this pet-masking spray. When I'm done cleaning, you won't smell a thing."

They were so grateful: "Oh, thank you, thank you! Dear lord, we don't know what to do with those cats!"

But there was no such thing as petgard. I used water, like I always did. But the water actually made the smell of cat piss much worse. It brought the smell right to the surface.

The hippies called in to the office: "What is the deal with this pet-masking spray?"

The next time I came in to work, my boss had a cassette player out on his desk.

"Check this out," he said and played me the Van Halen demos. These were recordings Gene Simmons had made with the band in Los Angeles: "Women in Love," "Runnin' with the Devil." A bunch of their songs. Van Halen had come up on the party circuit in Pasadena—they went on to become the big band on the Sunset Strip—and no one who'd heard them had ever heard anyone playing like Eddie Van Halen.

"Holy shit," I said. "These are amazing!"

"They truly are," my boss said. "I had a feeling you'd love them. But you know what else? You're fired."

The second time I heard Van Halen, I had signed on to work on the line at a steel manufacturing shop. It was the kind of place where one guy drilled a hole in the metal, a belt carried that hole down the line, and another guy put in a rivet.

I fucking hated that job. I slacked off as much as I could, sneaking into the part of the shop where spare metal was stored, and I would sit on the ground and read Alice Cooper's memoir. I still have my old, tattered copy, though I also have one that Alice gave me much later.

"Never forget: I was more dangerous once than you were," he wrote on the title page. That book is still a treasured possession of mine.

But every day, I'd pull a shift in that shop. After work, I'd go over to a house where a band called the Soothsayers lived. The Soothsayers were a Deep Purple–type band—they played bluesy riff rock. I wrote lyrics for them. I wasn't playing in bands yet, but I thought it was cool to hear my lyrics, even if some other band was playing them. Plus, I was learning a ton. I heard a lot of new things in that house: The Cars had just come out. The Clash and the Pistols, who looked like punks but wrote songs that were really traditional, solid rock songs. Sex Pistols songs were just like Kinks songs, with flatted thirds and flatted sevenths, like the Kinks used to play.

This was around the time that Van Halen's first album appeared. I was there when the Soothsayers first played it.

"Runnin' with the Devil" was the album's first song.

"Eruption" was second.

"Eruption" was an insane revelation. Ritchie Blackmore was still my favorite guitarist, but Blackmore could not have played what Eddie Van Halen was playing. It was so fast and so fluid. I was so happy, at that moment, not to have been a guitarist. Not to have been a technical player at all. But the Soothsayers' guitarist was holding his head in his hands.

"I quit," he said. "I quit."

He really meant it. A lot of guitarists heard that track and said, "I've got to figure out how to play like that." But this guitarist knew better. He said, "That's unattainable." And he really did quit. Just like that, it was the end of that band.

I had no interest in quitting. I wasn't a great player yet, but I was working hard to get there. I was studying. I was playing along with records, writing and playing my own melodies on top of songs, turning the chords around, writing my own chord progressions. I did everything I could do to improve as a songwriter, lyricist, and bass player. I wasn't just a teenager who had gone rogue. For everything that I did, I had a reason. If I stole, it was to fund something I *had* to do. Music, for me, was a form of survival. It was my purpose. It was bigger than me.

My wife says that I have a burning desire to master and conquer new things. "I can only imagine what it was like for you to be younger," she tells me.

I wasn't too different from the man she knows now. I was already compulsive. My personality was already immersive, addictive, engrossed. I had a dream, and I pursued my purpose to the exclusion of everything else.

I was, recognizably, who I am today.

Was I still living in Glendale? At some point, Don called me up: "Frankie. It's been months since you've paid the rent."

I said, "I'm trying!"

But I wasn't trying too hard. I spent all my money on amps, on equipment. I got an eviction notice but stayed on for a while after that, with the note on my door. After that, there were other, odd living arrangements. Rooms in guest houses. Weird little apartments. In Burbank, I lived in a converted garage and worked at Burbank Liquors, right on Burbank Boulevard. That liquor store is where I first met Mick Mars, who came in one night in an all-black outfit, with his black hair halfway down to his ass, and bought a half-pint of tequila.

Mick's real name is Bob Deal, and his stage name at the time was Zorky Charlamagne.

We looked at each other like two alley cats with their fur up.

"Do you play?" I asked.

"I'm a guitarist. You play?"

"I play some. What are you into?"

"Jeff Beck."

I liked Jeff Beck. My favorite album was *Blow by Blow*. For an instrumental album, it was a great rock-and-roll record.

"Paul Butterfield."

I said, "Who?" I'd never heard of Butterfield.

"What are *you* into?"

"Aerosmith. The New York Dolls. I like Joe Perry and Johnny Thunders."

"Okay," Mick said. "But if you want to hear a real guitar player, come down to the Stone Pony. My band, Spiders and Cowboys, is playing."

The Stone Pony was down the street from my garage. I got in somehow, though I was underage, and it changed me profoundly because Mick did a guitar solo using the mic stand as a slide. A few years later, I asked him about it.

"Sure," he said. "I remember."

"Can you do it on this song?" I had just written a song called "Piece of Your Action."

"I've got a whole part worked out," Mick said.

He played it, and it was amazing. Mick's fiercely proud of being a great guitarist. He might not talk about it at length, but he'll make sure you know it.

That night at the Stone Pony, we got drunk together and talked—I stumbled home to my garage and didn't see him again until the day he showed up to audition for Mötley Crüe. He'd put an ad in the *Recycler*: "Loud, rude, aggressive guitarist." We answered it, and Mick was as advertised. He was everything that we had been looking for. But it took the two of us a week before we realized that we'd met before back at the Stone Pony. I'd had long brown hair. Now, I had massively long, blue-black hair. Back then, we'd been Frankie and Zorky. Now we were Nikki and Mick.

Finally we put two and two together.

"Oh my God, you're that kid from the liquor store!"

"Oh my God, you're Zorky from Spiders and Cowboys!"

———

I was working a second job too, dipping circuit boards at a small factory. When I lost that job, I started taking the bus down to Hollywood and Vine to sweep the street out in front of Max Factor. The sidewalk had to be clean by the time the store opened, so I'd be awake before dawn. Then, in the back of the shop, I packed and stacked boxes of makeup. It was a weird, fuzzy time. After a few weeks or months in the converted garage, I moved to Hollywood, to an old house—a two-story, ramshackle, rotted-out band house, 6846 Sunset, directly across from Hollywood High School.

There were a million musicians who lived there. Kids sleeping on every couch, on the floors, in the closets, in the bushes outside. No one cleaned or cleared anything, ever. If bottles got kicked over, they stayed that way—all the way up to the day that whole place burned down, but we'll get to that part of the story.

There were punks who lived at 6846, hard rock kids, kids who were probably listening to Gary Numan and waiting for A Flock of Seagulls to come along. Once, I saw a check on the kitchen counter.

I picked it up; it was a publishing check, the first one I had ever seen. It was for eight cents, or maybe a quarter—whatever it was, it was less than a dollar.

I recall thinking, "Wow, one of my roommates must be a professional."

I also recall thinking, "Is there some way I could cash this?"

I still went back to Burbank and Glendale all the time. My girlfriend, Katie, lived in Glendale, at the top of a very steep hill. Even when my car was running, I'd have to drive it backward up that hill because there wasn't enough compression in the Buick's motor to do it the right way around. I'd put a towel on the floor next to the passenger seat—the floorboard had rotted through there—and we'd go back down the hill, very slowly, with me pumping the brakes the whole way.

I spent all the money I had on clothes, on pot, on equipment. After a few months, I'd saved enough to buy an Ampeg SVT tube bass head that year and an SVT-810 cabinet.

I was finally ready to go on auditions.

The *Recycler* was full of ads in those days: "Band into Cheap Trick, Aerosmith, and Mott the Hoople seeks bassist."

I'd go, "That's me!"

I'd pack all my equipment. My old Buick would be scraping the ground. Then I'd get to wherever the band was, unload.

Guitarists are lucky. Guitars don't weigh much. Guitar amps aren't as heavy as an SVT. Everything bassists use weighs a lot more. Bassists and drummers spend half their time hauling gear.

But I'd unload the stuff, knock on the door, and some old, bald guy would answer. The drummer looked like he belonged in a new wave band. The guitarist had long hair and looked like treasurer of the local Jimmy Page fan club.

Or it would be some old hippies. "Crosby, Stills & Nash seek their Neil Young" would have made for a more honest ad. And even if the guys looked cool enough, I'd set up, and they'd say, "Foreigner. 'Cold as Ice.'"

"Okay," I'd say. "How does it go?"

I had no interest in playing some other band's songs. But that's all anyone ever wanted to play, because they all had their eyes on the top-forty circuit. On that circuit, you had to play Donna Summer. You had to play Zeppelin. You had to take audience requests and anticipate what different audiences wanted to hear. Mick Mars was a part of that scene. That's how he became a monster guitarist, playing in a band called Whitehorse. Whitehorse played four sets a night, and he had to know four sets of music. It was like being a Beatle in Hamburg; you had to play everything, and you got good. But I wasn't interested in "everything."

"I want to play some of my own stuff," I'd say. "I have cool ideas."

"We don't do original music. There's no money in it."

Or I'd keep my mouth shut and play along:

"Foreigner. 'Cold as Ice.'"

"Sure. Count it off."

"Dude. What is that? That's not what the bassist is doing."

"I'm doing it like me," I'd say, and that would be the end of the audition.

It got to the point where I wouldn't even unload my equipment. I'd drive down to the audition. I'd get out of the car. But I wouldn't bother with my gear unless I was sure it was going to be worth it.

It never was, until I met Blackie and Lizzie and Dane.

London Calling

Chapter 14

Blackie Lawless was a man on a mission. He had been raised in the church, so he understood hymns and harmony singing. He had a strong sense of melody. He loved the Beatles, but you wouldn't have guessed it by looking at him. Blackie was a coarse-looking, gigantic man, big enough to have considered a career as a baseball player at one point. But now he dressed all in black, and his visual aesthetic was decadent, gruesome: Alice Cooper meets the Dolls. Blackie had actually played in the Dolls, filling in for Johnny Thunders when Thunders quit in the middle of one of their tours. Blackie played guitar alongside Sylvain Sylvain on the Dolls' last couple of shows.

This was all on the East Coast. But Blackie and the Dolls' bassist, Arthur Kane, had gone west and formed Killer Kane (which was Arthur Kane's nickname). That band released one EP. It went nowhere, and when Arthur went back to New York, Blackie stayed in LA and formed Sister.

I was burned out on auditions already. A few weeks earlier, in August, I had gone out to a house. The band looked cool, and their *Recycler* ad had said all the right things—but the singer was crying.

I said, "What happened?"

"You haven't heard?"

"I guess not . . ."

"Elvis died."

I said, "Yeah. Okay. So? Are we going to do the audition?"

"What's wrong with you, man? Elvis Presley just died!"

"What are you talking about?" I said. "Are we gonna rock? Or are we not gonna rock?"

"Dude, you don't get it."

"I get it," I said. "I just don't give a fuck."

Blackie was like me. Later on, he found religion or found his way back to religion. But by that point he'd long since formed W.A.S.P. and faced off with Tipper Gore and the Parents Music Resource Center, which went after Blackie for his song "Animal (Fuck Like a Beast)." The Blackie I knew then did not give a damn—and for what it's worth, he was right not to. Tipper went after Mötley Crüe too. She didn't like our song "Bastard." Our feeling then was, "Well, fuck you, but thank you," because the parental warning stickers the PMRC forced on us actually increased the sales of our albums.

Blackie was two years older than me, at a time when two years made a difference. He had actually *been in the Dolls*. He was a solid songwriter. In a perfect world, "Mr. Cool," the song he'd done with Killer Kane, would have been a big hit. But there wasn't really a place yet for music that mixed punk, glam, and hard rock with pop played the way that the Raspberries and Cheap Trick played it. That was the music I heard in my head. It's the reason I passed my audition. But Sister felt right, right away, anyway, not only because of Blackie but because Lizzie, Dane, and I felt an immediate connection.

Lizzie was so thin, his hip bones stuck out. He had dark hair and wore high-waisted pants that he tucked into high boots—it made him look elastic, like Gumby. He wore tube tops, which made his knobby shoulders and skinny arms look that much knobbier and skinnier. If you caught him from just the right angle, he looked like a witch, with his big nose and wide, goofy grin. He was delightful. He had a way with words—he had all these stock phrases, from Shakespeare or poetry, that he'd pull out—and he was mischievous and quick-witted. He wasn't into prose the way I was into it. He didn't read too much fiction. But he'd gotten those phrases from somewhere. He thought a lot about lyrics. He leaned toward Ian Hunter. He leaned toward Lou Reed. He was the first guy I ever wrote with, and we bounced ideas around until dawn or until one of us passed out first.

Dane was like a blond god next to Lizzie. He was perfectly proportioned; from a distance, you couldn't tell if he was five foot ten, five foot eight, or six foot three. Then you got closer and closer, and when you were standing next to him, you saw he was six foot four and almost comically handsome. Dane's jawline was perfectly square—almost too square for rock and roll. He belonged in Halston ads, not in makeup in a rock band. But that was his look. Because of it, you might have assumed that Dane was just another dumb blond.

He wasn't. Dane was probably smarter than Lizzie and me. He was certainly the voice of reason, the friend who'd say, "Maybe you don't want to throw that bottle?"

Or, "Are you *really* going to punch that guy? I mean, come on!"

Dane never acted like he had much to prove. He was solid. But he got the joke: this was rock and roll. It was rebellion. It was youth. It was *supposed* to be stupid and fun. To this day, he chuckles when I bring up all the old stories—because he knew *then* that we were ridiculous. He knew it long before we did. I don't know that Lizzie ever realized he was ridiculous. It only came crashing down on me in the last decade, how ridiculous I had once been. But Dane seemed to know all along.

Not for the first time, but for the first time in LA, I felt like I had found my people.

I was still living across from Hollywood High School, but that house burned down. Luckily, I wasn't home and my amp and my bass were at the pawnshop when the fire started. I had quit the steel manufacturing shop by then and gotten a job as a clerk at Wherehouse Records, but the job only paid minimum wage. It was impossible to keep my car running, so I'd started pawning equipment. When the work week was done, I'd walk to the blood bank, give blood, and between the check from my job and the money I got for my blood, I'd have just enough to get my stuff out of hock. Then I'd get a ride out to another audition.

Every couple of weeks, I'd repeat the whole cycle.

Slowly, but not surely, I made enough money to buy a new car—a '59 Volkswagen that wasn't in much better shape than the Buick had been. I only paid a hundred bucks for it. I didn't even bother getting it registered.

The cops didn't care in the seventies. They still didn't care in the eighties. On the day that I cashed my first publishing check for Mötley Crüe, I took the $6,000 and went out, immediately, to buy a new car. I got a black Porsche 914. I didn't have money left over for tax and registration and had to call Nona and Tom—who had no money themselves—and ask them for a loan. (That must have taken some nerve, though I made sure to pay them back quickly.) But that Porsche was the first car I owned that didn't break down all the time and could actually make it up every hill in Los Angeles County. It was a drop top, and after the Rainbow and Roxy and Whisky all closed, I'd race it down Sunset Boulevard.

The Porsche was a stick shift, of course, and one night I had Tommy in the car and Blackie was with us. I'm six foot one. Tommy's six foot three. Blackie's bigger than Dane—and a Porsche 914 is a two-seater about the size of a Miata. I don't know how we all fit, but we did. We had a bottle of Jack and a bottle of vodka, and we were going well over one hundred miles per hour when a black-and-white pulled up behind us.

The cops made us get out. We were dressed in black leather and not so steady on our feet.

The cops said, "Look, guys. You've got to slow down. And you're going to have to dump that alcohol out and drive safely. Please, go home now. And be careful."

If it had been Mom, driving with one of her Black or Latino boyfriends, it probably would have been a different story. But in those days, LA was pretty free-for-all. I got away with a lot. Looking back now, I can see that I was always working, always hustling, always on the make. But I don't believe I recognized, at the time, that I was poor, overworked, on my own. What I remember much more vividly is walking down Hollywood Boulevard with Lizzie and Dane. *Star Wars* had just come out, and there were *Star Wars* posters and billboards all over the place. Capezio shoes were a big deal at the time, and I had a pair of white Capezios. I had white bell-bottoms that laced up in the front and the back. I had a white T-shirt I'd cropped to show off my stomach. I had long brown hair. I felt like a rock star already, strutting around with my two mates who felt like rock stars themselves.

I recall looking down at the stars: Ingrid Bergman, Rita Hayworth, Jayne Mansfield, Yul Brynner. People I knew from TV, who had all come to Hollywood with the same dream.

———

We had a cheap rehearsal space down in Long Beach. The first time I drove out there, the four of us played "Mr. Cool"—and that was that. We were a band. It was everything I had ever wanted. Dane had a crazy drum kit by North Drums—all the toms were tube-shaped, huge and futuristic, and incredibly loud. It wasn't hard to lock into the rhythm. It would have been difficult not to, and even though I was still rough around the edges, I rode the pocket like my life depended on it.

Certainly all my fantasies did.

Afterward, we went to Blackie's apartment, where I was introduced to Thunderbird, along with Mad Dog 20/20—fortified, high-proof wines. If you want to know how bad alcohol can really be, a sip of either of those will give you an idea. A few more sips, and you've entered a dangerous place. But it became a routine: rehearsal, and then Blackie's place for some drinks. One night, Dane almost died John Bonham–style, throwing up while he was asleep.

All four of us had passed out. Dane was on Blackie's loveseat, surrounded by the fifty-five-gallon chemical drums Blackie used to drill out and put heating elements in. That was how Blackie paid the rent, making fog machines for other bands. He had green shag carpeting too and was passed out on the floor when Dane vomited all over him.

Blackie's hair was almost like a shampoo advertisement, fanned out all over the shag. Except now his hair, the rug, and a few other things were all covered in puke. When Dane finally woke up and saw what he'd done, he ran right out of the apartment. I would have run too: Blackie was intimidating. We were all tall—whether or not we were in heels, we'd walk into the Rainbow and make an impression. But Blackie was from Staten Island. He was bigger and older and tougher than us, and he'd throw his weight around if and when he felt it was called for.

At rehearsal, he turned to Dane once and said, "Play it like this."

Dane said, "Okay," and he tried playing his part Blackie's way. But whatever Blackie had asked him to do wasn't working.

"I'm going to play it my way," Dane said.

"No. Play it my way."

"No. I'm playing it like this . . ."

After a few rounds of this, Blackie asked him, "Do you want to step outside?"

Dane and Blackie stepped out. Lizzie shrugged. He and I stared at each other. Five minutes later, Dane and Blackie came back.

They were laughing. Later that week, Dane told us what Blackie had said. "I'm thinking we're gonna scrap, right? So, okay, I'm getting ready. But Blackie goes, 'Look, we got into this for the same reasons, right? We just want to get laid. Will you work with me here?' He didn't want to fight. He just wanted to convince me to do it his way."

That was Blackie in a nutshell. When you looked at him, you saw a menacing guy. When you listened to him, you heard menacing songs. But Blackie sitting out on the beach somewhere, playing Beatles tunes on an acoustic guitar and singing the harmony parts—that's the real, inner Blackie the world has never seen. Later on, when I did "Shout at the Devil," I think he got pissed. How could he not have been? I had taken stuff from him. I had taken Mötley Crüe's penta-gram from Blackie. He wasn't using it anymore—and I had asked his permission. But I did take it. Lighting myself on fire was a Blackie move too. I never saw him do it, but he'd talk about throwing worms out into the audience. He'd talk about pouring lighter fluid all over himself. Blackie was always trying to come up with some new way to shock. By the time I met him, he'd decided, "I'm not doing any of that anymore." But he'd tell me about it, and I'd think, "Really? In that case, I will!" And I did. In Mötley's apartment, we'd practice: Vince and Tommy would douse me in lighter fluid—and, obviously, we had shag carpeting too. It's a miracle we didn't all burn to death.

Blackie understood where I was coming from. But I think he couldn't help being pissed. I understood where he was coming from too.

———

We rehearsed for three or four weeks at the most. It could have even been two or three. Then it was time to make our demo. That was something Blackie knew how to do, but the rest of us were incred-ibly green. We had no experience at all. We'd never been inside a studio.

We sucked—and, in a way, it was the best thing that could have happened to us. There was never any question that Sister was Blackie's band. Blackie had put it together. Blackie sang and wrote all the songs. If Blackie didn't like what we were playing behind him, he wasn't shy about letting us know. It's not like we had been tricked: we all knew going in that, if we were with Blackie, it was going to be his operation. But at some point, I am sure, I would have bristled. I had already amassed ten or twelve songs. Lizzie was writing stuff too and chomping at the bit. Dane had his own ideas about the way he wanted to play. Sooner or later, we were going to butt heads. But that moment came sooner than we expected it to because as soon as Blackie heard what we had recorded, he fired the three of us.

Just like that, right then and there: "You're all out. We're history. We're not doing this."

It stung, but there was an upside: there was much more room for Lizzie, Dane, and me to do our own things.

We didn't have to talk or even think about staying together. We just placed an ad in the *Recycler* and started auditioning singers.

We decided to call ourselves London because London was where all the best bands were from.

The Spotlight

Chapter 15

W e got a rehearsal space above a gay bar called the Spotlight, which stood on the corner of Selma and Cahuenga, a few blocks away from the Hollywood Walk of Fame. The room was tiny—it was like rehearsing in the back of a U-Haul—but we kept the same space for as long as I was in London. A band called the Mau Maus rehearsed in the one right next door. Six nights a week, starting at six, we'd play for six hours straight. Then we'd spill into the hallway, say hi to the Mau Maus, have a few drinks, shoot the shit. Without fail, the Mau Maus were always dressed in black leather. They were all super skinny, they wore caps like SS officers would wear, and there was some skittish but obvious drug stuff going on that they only half hid from us.

I thought those guys were on a whole other level. They listened to us, and we listened to them. We went to see them play a few times in some underground club. They were carving a different niche for themselves, but if there was anyone I could steal from or be inspired by, I would be paying attention.

The gay thing was new to me too. If there was a gay scene in Idaho, it must have been buried deep underground. But the Spotlight's doors opened right onto a busy corner, and the crowd always spilled outside the bar. We thought it was cool. It reminded us of Bowie and the New York Dolls. Anything that felt transgressive, we liked. But we didn't go into the actual bar, not so much because we were underage (no one cared) or because we were straight (no one cared) but because we were so poor. We'd split bottles of Bacardi instead. Each of us got cans of soda. We swigged the Bacardi and chased it with Coke until the whole bottle was gone. That was our ritual: six hours of practice, and then we'd go out for the night. It became such a part of my brain and my wiring that when I went to get my first tattoo, I asked for Bacardi's bat emblem. Robert Benedetti was the guy who gave it to me. He was the first guy I'd seen with pierced nipples. The first guy I saw with tattoos on his hands. These days, I have so many tattoos, I'd have to look for a long while to find the bat Robert gave me. (For reasons I can no longer remember, he added a moon.) At the time, I was very impressed.

There was a listing in the *Recycler:* a cheap room in an old art deco building. Seventy bucks. I could just about afford it even before I got Dane, who had been sleeping in his car, to move in and split the cost. The apartment belonged to a photographer who only shot black-and-white film. He slept in the bedroom while Dane and I took turns on the living room couch.

Our building was full of old people who looked like they'd been there since World War I. They were always falling, maybe dying—ambulances pulled up at all hours, sirens blaring. Or they got stuck in the elevators, which were always stopping a little below or above the thresholds they should have been stopping at. But the rent was right, and Craig, the photographer, was talented and laid back. The photos he took were all super-grainy and chic.

Just then, I was reading Ian Hunter's *Diary of a Rock 'n' Roll Star*, which became an inspiration for my book *The Heroin Diaries*. There's a scene in Hunter's book that I found striking. He's talking about how the whole band is British, they're not getting a whole lot of sun, but now here they are, sitting poolside at a Tropicana in some sunny place. He describes the guitarist's stacked boots, and the drummer's got stars on his jeans.

Our apartment was high above the sidewalk, and we could see over the neighboring houses. Down at the end of the block, there was a building with a swimming pool. I told Dane that if we could get Craig to shoot us around that pool, it would look just like that scene.

We had to jump a few fences to get there. But one day we got all rocked out. We had five guys in the band at that time, and we made our way over. Just as we were arranging ourselves around the pool, we saw a dude running toward us carrying a Louisville Slugger.

We ran out through the lobby with this maniac swinging the bat right behind us. Just as we reached the far door, he lifted it high and took a giant swing. Instead of hitting us, he hit a glass chandelier. The crystals shattered, glass fell all around us, and the guy swung again—he must have been some sort of madman. You could see in his eyes that he had a screw loose. He would have killed us or beaten us within an inch of our lives, but we were so startled and scared, it didn't even occur to us to rush him.

Why didn't the five of us tackle him? He was just one guy. But he was determined. We were determined too, but he had a baseball bat, and all we had was our band.

———

Dane got a job cleaning pools: Beverly Hills. Bel Air. All the houses were mansions. If I had time off work, I'd go with him.

One of the accounts Dane had was James Caan's.

Caan had a huge house—if memory serves, he'd bought it from Carl Wilson of the Beach Boys. But Dane had inherited the James Caan account. Caan didn't know what we looked like, and while we were working, he ran out of the house, screaming and swinging a rope like a lasso that he just happened to have because he was a movie star and movie stars had all been issued lassoes at some point.

It was very strange, like a replay of what had happened to us with the Louisville Slugger. We must have looked strange to James Caan. Two dudes who were not wearing board shorts and Hawaiian shirts, like you'd expect pool cleaners to wear. By this point, my rock clothes were just the clothes that I dressed in—I didn't have any others—and Dane was wearing his own rock-and-roll outfit.

Caan screamed for a while. He swung his lasso. Finally, he calmed down. The funny thing was, Dane had that account for a while, and Caan stiffed him and stiffed him. When Dane cornered him and forced him to promise to pay, Caan had his accountant send a check that wasn't signed. Dane sent it back, and the accountant sent out another—but on this check, the bank account number would be smudged and unreadable.

This went on, and it went on. It kept going. It became a big hassle. James Caan was a movie star. He had a lasso. He had a mansion in Beverly Hills. The only thing he didn't have was the $45 he owed Dane for cleaning his pool.

Somewhere in there, we felt, was a valuable lesson. But I'm not sure we knew what it was.

All three of us got a job selling light bulbs somewhere around Sunset Boulevard. The office we worked out of is a recording studio now—I've heard that one of the guys from Devo owns it. Back then, it was a bunch of cubicles, each with a chair, an old phone, a phone book, and nothing else. Every morning we'd start making cold calls, trying to sell the bulbs for two or three times what they were worth. It was purely a numbers game: if we made enough calls, someone was bound to say yes. That one person covered the cost of the rest of the calls.

I'd pick a name out of the phone book. "Bob Archibald?" I'd give Bob the name of the company we worked for. It was official-sounding, and sometimes it worked.

"Tell me, Bob. How many light fixtures do you have? Sixteen? I see. Are any of them black around the edges? Because if they are, they'll catch fire. You got any bulbs that are out? That can be dangerous too."

Every day we wrote out some orders. Then Lizzie got an idea.

"Why are we working for someone else? Why don't we start our own company?"

We came up with GEL—General Electric Light. It was completely unregistered and illegal, but we came up with a logo, bought some jumpsuits, and had T-shirts made. We made some cold calls and showed up ourselves an hour later with a bunch of light bulbs. We'd take all the customer's old light bulbs. Then we'd sell those light bulbs on down the line.

The scam actually worked. We opened a business account at a bank. No one there asked for ID.

Lizzie got a magnet made that read "General Electric Light." He stuck it to the side of his shitty old car, and he'd pull up in his ratty gray jumpsuit. All three of us used fake names. I was Nick Johnson. Dane used the name of the guy who was booking a club called Starwood: "I'm David Forrest," he'd say. Lizzie used his actual name, which was Steve Perry. He didn't like that name because of the other Steve Perry, who was the singer in Journey. But for our company, it was just right.

Then Lizzie had one more idea. He'd call someone who had bought from us previously, using a voice that was off, maybe stoned or just slow. He would speak *very* slowly, as if daring the customer to hang up on him. Inevitably, it would happen. The customer would hang up. Then, using his actual voice, he'd call back.

"Hi, this is Steve Perry from GE Supply. I'm just calling to confirm your order of twelve eight-foot Watt-Misers."

The customer would freak out. "What? I didn't order any at all."

The customer would fume. He'd sputter. Without fail, he'd say, "Some idiot called me, but I didn't order any goddamned light bulbs."

Lizzie would pause. He'd look very serious, even though Dane and I would both be making faces at him. Then he'd say, "You know what? I'm really sorry. But that guy's messed up for the last time. I'm firing his ass. He's done. It's not my problem whether he lives or eats."

All of a sudden, the customer would soften. "You know what?" he'd say. "Go ahead. Put it through. The guy was fine; I don't mean to get him in trouble."

Lizzie was that kind of thinker. His mischievous streak came through in everything he did. It was there in his writing, in his guitar playing. It was there in the way he strutted down Hollywood Boulevard in a tube top. He was a pleasure just to be around.

Nikki Nine

Chapter 16

The Doors had been the house band at the Whisky a Go Go—at least they were until Jim Morrison started singing about wanting to screw his own mother. Buffalo Springfield premiered at the Troubadour. The Byrds were the house band down the street at Ciro's. Gazzarri's on La Cienega had had a house band led by Edward James Olmos, the actor. The owner—Gazzarri himself—liked to dress up in wide-lapel pinstripe suits, like an old-school Chicago-style gangster. The Sunset Strip is where the sixties had happened in Los Angeles. It's where the best record stores were and the clothing boutiques that catered to mods and hippies. There were music stores, record labels, studios: Sunset Sound, Western Recorders, A&M, RCA (where the Stones recorded "Satisfaction"). The strip even had its own riots, which broke out in 1966 when thousands of kids went wild to protest a ten o'clock curfew the city was trying to enforce. That's what Buffalo Springfield's best-known song was about—not Vietnam or anything to do with civil rights. "For What It's Worth" was a protest song about the Sunset Strip riots.

Even the hotels on Sunset were famous. The Chateau Marmont and Hyatt House, which everyone called the Riot House. Keith

Moon and Keith Richards threw TVs off the balconies there. John Bonham rode a Harley up and down the halls. Every rock star shenanigan you can imagine—and some you probably can't—took place on a regular basis.

When Motown moved out of Detroit, the company moved into an office on Sunset. The Rainbow opened in 1972. Rodney Bingenheimer's English Disco became a home away from home for British expats: David Bowie, Elton John, John Lennon, Mick Jagger. Even the groupies at Rodney Bingenheimer's were famous. The Roxy opened in 1973. Then, in 1974, Van Halen started their regular gig at Gazzarri's.

Van Halen was the biggest backyard party band in Pasadena when Eddie and Alex were still in high school. Whenever they played, the whole school would show up. But Gazzarri's was Van Halen's Hamburg: the place where they played three or four sets a night and got as tight as they ever would be.

By the time I arrived in Hollywood, they had outgrown the clubs. Van Halen had gone from Gazzarri's to bigger venues, like the Starwood, to opening up for Black Sabbath, to coheadlining with Aerosmith. But they had been such a strong part of the scene for so long that their absence was still noticeable: it felt more like a thing than a void. Afterward, the scene splintered. You had old-school punks. You had the new punks, coming in from Orange County. You had the first stirrings of new wave. The biggest band playing hard rock in the clubs now was easily Quiet Riot.

Quiet Riot was Randy Rhoads's band. After Eddie Van Halen, Rhoads was the most interesting, most innovative guitarist in Los Angeles. Both of Randy's parents were music teachers. When Randy's father walked out on the family, his mother opened a music school to pay the rent. Randy was her best student. He played classical guitar, which you can hear if you listen closely to his solos. He studied theory. He took lessons for just one year before his guitar teacher announced that there wasn't anything left to teach him.

Randy was tiny and blond, like a pixie. He wore polka dots, vests, and bow ties, and I would push my way to the front whenever Quiet Riot played and stare, slack-jawed, at what he was doing.

Quiet Riot's singer was excellent too. Kevin DuBrow loved Steve Marriott and the Small Faces. Marriott had one of the great rock-and-roll voices—Jimmy Page had wanted him for Led Zeppelin before settling for Robert Plant—but DuBrow didn't embarrass himself when he did his best to imitate Marriott. He had a hell of a voice of his own.

We paid close attention to Quiet Riot, and I spent some time with the guys in the band.

Randy and I never became fast friends. But we'd hang out at the Starwood, where Quiet Riot was the top act. We played Asteroids together. We drank Randy's drink of choice, gin and tonics. We drank a lot of them. The hangovers were intense, but getting to spend time with Randy was worth it. We also played music together—not often, but from time to time. I'd drive my Volkswagen out to Burbank, where Randy still lived with his mother. I'd have my SVT head and my SVT cabinet, and Randy's mom would help us roll it up the driveway and into his bedroom. Randy had a Jimi Hendrix poster, a twin mattress down on the floor, and an amp—it may have been a small Fender Reverb—that he'd turned to face the wall.

"Why'd you do that with your amp?" I asked him.

"I like the sound that comes out of the back."

Quiet Riot had made two albums, but those albums had only come out in Japan. It didn't seem to matter how big they were on the scene: American labels had all turned their backs on hard rock. Guitars were on their way out. Synths were in. But Randy played me his albums, and I was impressed. They were solid, or better than solid. Quiet Riot had a great song called "Slick Black Cadillac." Randy taught me how to play it. I showed him the songs I had been writing too. Then, with his mother, we'd sit down to eat. But in the back of my mind, I was gunning for Randy, gunning for Kevin, gunning for Quiet Riot's spot at the top.

It must have been 1978, because 1978 was the year I met Quiet Riot's bassist, Rudy Sarzo. In fact, I am sure, because to this day Rudy and I have the same nickname for one another: "Seventy-Eight."

But in 1978, I had almost taken Rudy's spot.

Kevin DuBrow bumped into me at the Starwood and asked me to come to his place the next day. I did, and I was surprised to see how posh it was. No one I knew at the time had an apartment half as nice as Kevin's. I didn't know it at the time, but DuBrow had family money. He had good furniture and a fancy stereo with the biggest speakers I'd ever seen.

In the seventies, we used to sit on the floor to listen to music. So we sat on the floor and listened to Slade, Sweet, Bad Company, and some Steve Marriott stuff. Kevin played me a few songs off his Japanese albums. Then he said, "Listen, we're thinking of getting rid of our bass player . . ."

I turned him down flat. He ended up hiring Rudy.

Today I think, "He had a record deal. Why did I pass?"

Kevin was such a good singer. He laid it all out on the line, and his band had the greatest guitar player this side of Eddie Van Halen. I was a hayseed, straight off the bus from Idaho.

But even then, I had thought, "I have ideas of my own."

I think that Kevin turned on me then. The fact that his next band, DuBrow, opened for Mötley Crüe didn't help either. Later on, after Randy had passed away and Kevin had reformed Quiet Riot, he wouldn't stop saying nasty things about me and Mötley, especially in the press.

I don't take that sort of thing lying down. I hit DuBrow back where I knew it would hurt.

From the day I met him (and, I imagine, for quite a while before that), Kevin had been losing his hair. He'd used weird stuff that came in a can to make it look like his hair wasn't patchy and thinning—but it always backfired because, on stage, under the lights, all this black stuff would start running down his face.

When he started slagging me off in the press and I got calls to respond, I'd just talk about Kevin's hair. He was bitter because he was balding, I'd say.

We were both assholes, I guess. Then again, as my Uncle Don could have told me, it's not show friends—it's show business. Today, I am grateful to Kevin. When London was just starting out, we'd see Quiet Riot playing the Starwood, selling the place out on weekends, and tell ourselves, "Man, someday, maybe we could do that. We could have that, someday, for our band." Randy and Kevin had set the bar high.

———

It was around that same time that I moved in with Angie, who was writing and singing in a band called Tripper and studying journalism at USC. I had auditioned for Tripper, driving down to Hawthorn with my Fender bass and all my gear, only to find that I disliked the guitarist. He had curly hair, and I was firmly of the opinion that curly hair had no place in rock and roll. Worse than his hair, he liked Rush—he wanted that thin, busy, Rickenbacker-ish bass sound. I hated Rush. I liked a bass sound that was fat and thick, with tons of bottom.

Actually, I hate Rush to this day. I get that they're talented guys. But I might ask you, "Do you like Rush?"

If I do, you should say, "No." Otherwise, we're probably not going to have much of a relationship.

But Angie and I hit it off. We hated the same bands. We liked the same bands. We liked the same clothes. We teased our hair the same way. When my house on Hollywood Boulevard burned down, I moved into her apartment on Beachwood Drive. First, there were three of us: Angie; Lisa, her roommate; and me. But Lisa and I didn't get along either—it was like a repeat of my interactions with Angie's guitarist, except that I didn't have to play in his band. I did have to live with Lisa. Day in and day out, she was there.

I liked the apartment. I liked Beachwood Canyon, which was full of musicians, writers, artists, actors on the make. It was pretty clear: Lisa would have to go, or Angie and I would have to move out. But that situation took care of itself when I decided to dye my hair black in the bathtub.

I had a lot of hair—it took a lot of dye—and that black dye got all over the place.

"This is so disgusting," Lisa said when she came home. "This is just so . . . disgusting."

I told her, "If you don't like it, you don't have to stay."

There was some screaming, and Lisa may have broken a few of our dinner plates on her way out. But that was the last I saw of her.

Angie and I went on double dates with Lizzie and his girlfriend— who was also named Lisa. I couldn't get away from the Lisas. We'd go down to Rainbow, where Joe DiMaggio and Marilyn Monroe had their first date, or go in on a bottle and walk the length of the strip. We went out to shows and stayed up half the night afterward doing postmortems. When Aerosmith played a private show, billed as Dr. J Jones and the Interns, we were there. Afterward, I sketched the whole thing on a series of cocktail napkins: where Steven Tyler and Joe Perry had stood, how they'd moved, all the things they could have done to have gotten even more out of the stage. I was always thinking, always strategizing, always out at the clubs.

Angie was always out too, because she was writing about bands for the *Anaheim Bulletin*.

One of those bands was Squeeze—Squeeze, the cover band from California, not the pop band from England. Angie had dated the front man, Jeff Nicholson. She had designed the band's logo, which I saw while flipping through one of her scrapbooks. I thought she had done a great job, drawing a guy in Kiss-like makeup squeezing a woman in his hand like King Kong squeezing Fay Wray.

Squeeze was from Riverside. I had never been to Riverside or heard of Squeeze. But I was interested and asked a few questions.

Jeff sang and played bass. He had come up playing in cover bands with Sammy Hagar.

Then, Angie said, he and Sammy had gone their separate ways. Jeff formed Squeeze and gave himself a stage name: Niki Syxx.

I loved that name right away—even though it was missing that sweet extra *k*. Then and there, I decided to steal it.

For a while, I went around calling myself Nikki London. But it caused problems, eventually, because of what we called the "Van Halen Syndrome." London wasn't my band in the way that Sister was Blackie's. London was more of a democracy, and unless Lizzie, Dane, and I did what the Ramones had done—unless Lizzie and Dane changed their last names to London as well—it was going to be hard to avoid the impression that the whole thing was my band and not everyone's band.

I needed to do something quickly. We were starting to get better shows on better nights at bigger places. We could feel ourselves gaining on Randy and Kevin and everyone else on the strip.

There was no doubt in my mind: we were going to be huge.

I thought about it for a while. "Nikki Nine" was on the table briefly. I liked the way Nikki Nine sounded: tough and punk rock.

Then I thought, "Fuck it."

"Okay," I told Angie, "I'm just going to be Nikki Sixx."

"Frank!" she said. "You can't just *be Nikki Sixx*! That's *Jeff's* stage name."

"Whatever," I said. "He's never going to make it."

Niki Syxx

Chapter 17

I was right. Squeeze didn't make it. They couldn't have, because, in 1979, Jeff became a born-again Christian.

I've heard that he's living in Oregon now, playing his Christian music, spreading the gospel, and bemoaning his old, wicked rock-and-roll ways. Jeff thinks rock and roll is the devil's music. He thinks that me stealing his name is the least of my sins and my problems and that, undoubtedly, I am going to hell anyway.

There's even a pamphlet that Jeff once put out: "Confession of a Rocker, by Niki Syxx."

"My Name is Niki Syxx . . . What???" it begins.

> Isn't Nikki Sixx the bass player for Mötley Crüe? Yes, he is. But his real name is Frank, and my real name is Jeff. So how did we end up with the same stage name? Well, years ago, before Mötley Crüe was formed, I was in a popular Southern California band named "Squeeze" and I had decided that my name was just too plain and I needed a stage name. Since my last name is Nicholson, I thought I would call myself "Niki," but I couldn't think of a last name to go with it. Then one day as I was driving in Newport Beach, I saw the name Niki 6 on a license plate of a Mercedes . . . so, for the next five years of my life I was "Niki Syxx."

Then, Niki says, I met Angie.

> A few years later Frank started dating a girl who had earlier taken
> pictures of Squeeze. One day he opened her photo album, saw the
> pictures and took an interest in my stage name. After finding out
> that I wasn't playing music at the time, he decided to use it for
> himself. He later acknowledged this in a *BAM* magazine. In any
> case, he's welcome to the name, and I want to tell you why.

Well, kind of. Sort of . . .

Jeff and Angie had gone out with each other for more than a year,
so calling her "a girl" who had taken his picture is a bit misleading.
But Jeff's right: *I* never lied about any of it. If asked, I'd tell reporters,
"I, Nikki London, decided: not only was I going to take the guy's
girlfriend. I was also taking his name."

What of it? I had never heard of the guy until Angie showed me
her scrapbook. What did I care, and what did it matter? It wasn't like
I had stolen Johnny Thunders's name.

I'll be the first to admit it was shameless. But isn't *shameless* another
word for rock and roll?

Nigel

Chapter 18

London had a secret weapon. His name was John St. John.

John was a classically trained pianist, left-handed, and he played a Hammond organ through a Leslie cabinet. The combination of those three things gave us a low end that was louder and spookier sounding than anything else on the strip. It freed me to ride quarter notes much more deeply and lock in that much more closely with Dane.

John had an Orchestron too—one of the first sampling keyboards. The thing was a nightmare to work with. If you so much as looked at it, it went out of tune. But it sounded just like a pipe organ. It could also sound like a cello, flute, French horn, or full choir. It was very new, very expensive: in those days, most people used the Orchestron to score films. It was one more thing that set us apart.

We kept rehearsing, six hours a night. But we just couldn't find the right singer. We auditioned some real world-class stinkers and finally got to the point where Lizzie said, "I'm going to try."

"Me too," I said.

That was the first time I tried to sing lead instead of backup, and I was atrocious—even worse than the punk rockers. Then I tried singing harder, but my voice gave out.

Lizzie was better but not good enough, and we had to go back to auditioning singers. We had Steven Toth in the band for a minute. He'd been the singer in a group called Faze, which was a sort of prog-rock party band in the Valley. He had a distinctive high voice, and he was a good, solid guy. But Steve wasn't a big guy, and at the time, I had all sorts of rules about playing rock and roll. If you were diminutive, you had better be as good as Randy Rhoads. To be in a rock band, you had to have hair, but curly hair was a no-no. A band had to look a certain way, and in heels, Lizzie, Dane, and I were almost seven feet tall. Steve would have had to stand on stilts. We rehearsed and agreed, amicably, to part ways before playing together in public.

Then, through an ad in the *Recycler*, we found Henry Valentine.

Henry was older than us—twenty-nine, maybe thirty—and had much more musical experience. He understood music theory. He taught us a lot in terms of arranging, song structure, dynamics. But Henry was old enough to have been a real hippie, and he had remained a hippie—he was so much more laid back than we were. He wasn't hungry. He just didn't have any angst.

This was back in the days when the rest of us could go all day and all night without eating. Maybe, after rehearsal, we'd go down to the Rainbow and get girls to buy us drinks and pizza somewhere—and that's all we'd have for that day. We'd go home with this girl or that girl, stagger out of bed at three or four, make it to rehearsal by six, and at midnight we'd do the same thing again.

Angie and I were incredibly young. I cared for her. I did my best to be good to her, and she took good care of me. But times were different, and I was focused on so many things. Monogamy wasn't high on the list.

———

I worked night and day on our sets, our stage clothes, our songs. I wrote songs on my bass, on guitar. I rented a piano and used it to write Mott the Hoople–type stuff. I hustled hard to get gigs. We ended up at the Troubadour. We played more places in Orange County. We played dives on the outskirts of LA. We worked our way up to some dates at the Starwood: weekday slots, midnight slots, eight p.m. slots—terrible times. We kept doing them, eventually working our way up to weekends. I promoted us tirelessly. In those days, I'd go into a print shop and say, "What's the biggest-sized poster you have?"

They'd point to something that was too small.

"Is that it? Can't go bigger?"

"Well, I guess we can. But once you get past this point, the price doubles."

"How much?"

It's hard to recall exact figures, so let's just say the price for a thousand big posters was around one hundred bucks.

I'd say, "Okay. Let me think about that."

Then I'd go down to the next print shop.

"Hey. The shop down the block can make two-foot-by-three-foot posters. Can you?"

"I guess we can do that."

"Down the street, they said they'd give me a thousand for fifty bucks."

"Oh. Well. Gee. We could maybe do it for seventy-five?"

Seventy-five was a lot. Seventy-five was a full month's rent where I was living with Dane and Craig, the photographer, so I put an ad in the *Recycler*: "Upright piano for sale: $250."

That paid for a lot of posters, and I sunk the rest into the band.

I sunk everything into the band in those days. I sunk everything into Mötley Crüe too, for a long while after I formed it. All the money we made in those days went into better equipment and bigger PAs, into our stage sets, our clothes, our light rigs—whatever we could do to put on the best, biggest, most unforgettable show that had ever come through your town.

But a week after I'd sold the piano (which never had been mine to sell), a knock came on the door.

"Who is it?" Dane answered.

"Los Angeles Police."

I put my hand on Dane's shoulder. "I'm not home," I whispered.

But when Dane opened the door just a crack, the detectives just pushed their way in.

"We're looking for Frank Feranna."

"No one here by that name," I said.

"What's your name?"

"He's Dane. I'm Nikki Sixx."

"Where's Feranna?"

"Moved out. Didn't leave an address."

The police never did catch up to Frank—at least, not in regard to that piano. Craig wasn't too thrilled when he heard about that. But it was the next set of posters that got us evicted. For that set, I just used our rent money. For Craig, it was the last straw.

That was when I moved in with Angie, and Dane went back to sleeping in his car—a Volkswagen, like the one I had. It wasn't so comfortable for him, but it was worth it.

Tommy Lee had one of those big two-by-three-foot London posters up in his bedroom. He was just a kid, too young to get into the clubs, but he was a big London fan. Lots of kids were. Word got around, and after six or eight months of hustling, we finally got a good weekend time slot at the Starwood.

By then, we had all agreed to part ways with Henry Valentine.

It wasn't just that Henry was too laid back. It was also that he looked and sounded too much like Robert Plant and wanted to go in more mainstream directions. During the last rehearsal we'd had before a big show, we had decided together that this would be his last show with London.

Dane had already put an ad in the *Recycler*: "Looking for a singer influenced by David Bowie, Freddie Mercury, or Nigel Benjamin."

Nigel Benjamin was the singer who'd taken over from Ian Hunter in Mott the Hoople. It was Nigel Benjamin who had sung "No Such Thing as Rock and Roll"—a song that had blown Dane's mind, and Lizzie's, and mine. There are no vocal effects on that song. There's no harmonizer, no pitch transposer—those things hadn't been invented yet. It's a slow roll, but when the song opens up, Nigel does some astonishing things.

Ian Hunter was a bit like Bob Dylan, an amazing lyricist and songwriter. I'd listen to him and think of Burroughs and Bukowski. But Nigel Benjamin was an amazing *singer*—like David Bowie, except with more range. Plus, putting his name in the ad, and not Hunter's, seemed like a good way to separate the wheat from the chaff: if you knew who Nigel Benjamin was, you were bound to be serious.

So we played that last show with Henry. Afterward, we were backstage, and a guy came up to me.

He was a bit older and unshaven, and he wore an oversized sports coat.

"Hi," he said. "I'm Nigel."

"Nigel?"

"Nigel Benjamin."

I looked him up and down. He was English. He had the right accent. He wasn't a bad-looking guy. He was muscular, skinny. But his look was very *Miami Vice,* and *Miami Vice* wasn't a thing yet. To me, he just looked like a bum.

"Okay," I said, and I laughed. I turned my back to him and started talking to someone else.

But Dane kept looking at him. Something about this bum was ringing a bell with our drummer.

"I saw your ad," the guy told Dane. "You know, I thought I'd have a good chance."

Dane laughed.

"How many octaves can you sing?" he asked.

The guy blinked and looked at Dane with a bored, blank expression. "I sing them all, don't I?"

"I mean, how high can you sing?"

"I can sing as high as I want."

"But *how high*? I mean . . . on a guitar. How many notes that are on a guitar can you sing?"

"I can sing all the fuckin' notes."

There was no way this bum could have been Nigel. But Dane and Lizzie were halfway convinced—maybe more than halfway. They drove out to Venice Beach where the guy lived to make sure, and they came back astounded.

———

It was like some sort of dream, having the real Nigel Benjamin in our band. I thanked God I hadn't joined Quiet Riot.

We played a warm-up show at the arena, which was a small place. We didn't invite anyone—we just wanted to see for ourselves. We all thought we sounded like shit. It's hard, when you're starting out, to measure up to what you hear in rehearsal, where you're playing under much more controlled conditions and don't have to deal with a strange room, a strange stage, strange monitors, and someone else's PA. We all thought Nigel would be disappointed. But Nigel was like a kid in a candy store. He loved it. He said, "That was incredible. This is exactly what we need to do."

Nigel was a funny guy. He was twenty-six or twenty-seven years old, living in Venice with his German girlfriend, and I think they had a small kid. He'd been in a very big band and toured the world. I can see now that he was in a different place in his life. Sometimes he'd come to rehearsal elated. Sometimes he'd be the opposite—deflated, like a balloon. I suppose that, like a lot of creative types, Nigel was a bit manic-depressive. But we were excited just to be around him.

With Henry Valentine, we'd been gunning for Quiet Riot. With Nigel on our team, we started aiming much higher. We booked studio time. We recorded a demo. When Angie and I drove out to have dinner at her parents' house, all I could talk about was my demo. When we had dinner at Don and Sharon's, all I could talk about was my new name and my band. At rehearsal, I told the guys about Don: "My uncle's going to sign us, and we're going to be as big as Sweet."

Even Nigel had seemed impressed.

On our way out the door, I slipped Don a copy of our demo.

"Don," I said. "You've gotta come hear us play."

The Starwood

Chapter 19

Bill Gazzarri, who owned Gazzarri's, may have dressed like an old-school mobster, but Eddie Nash was the real deal: an actual gangster. He was a perpetually coked-up, paranoid, vicious, and violent man.

Nash owned the Kit Kat, a strip club on Santa Monica; the Soul'd Out, a Black club on Sunset; and the Odyssey, an all-ages club on Beverly. He owned the Paradise Ballroom, a gay club on North Highland, and the Seven Seas, a tiki bar and disco on Hollywood Boulevard. Ali Baba's, Nash's club on Sherman at Lankershim, had a Middle Eastern theme and belly dancers who worked for tips and probably did quite a bit more on the side—especially when groups of Saudis came through.

Eddie Nash also owned the Starwood, and the Starwood was now our second home. But we never dealt with him directly. We signed a management contract with David Forrest, who booked bands at the Starwood but had his own storied career. Forrest had worked with Bill Graham and David Geffen. He had managed Lindsey Buckingham and Stevie Nicks before Mick Fleetwood brought them into Fleetwood Mac. Forrest had managed Quiet Riot. He'd promoted shows with Kiss, Aerosmith, and other big acts. We didn't understand that he was on his way down in the business—to us, he was still a big deal. After we'd headlined a couple of times, packing the house every time, he pulled out a contract and gave it to us.

It was Quiet Riot's old contract. In fact, David just crossed out the words *Quiet Riot* and wrote *London* in by hand. That was some sort of dick power move. But we signed the papers and David put us to work—literally. By the end of the week, we were cleaning the club, running errands, and doing construction.

We didn't know what we were doing, especially when it came to construction. Lizzie had never held a hammer before. The Starwood's walls were wood paneled, and Gary Fontenot, who managed the club, told us to put new cedar up where the bathroom walls had rotted through. We put nails right through the plumbing. Water spurted everywhere. We strolled back out as if nothing had happened. After that, we stuck more to the janitorial side of the job.

Booking at the Starwood was totally schizophrenic. You'd have Fear playing one night, followed by the Plimsouls, followed by the Germs, followed by Gang of Four, followed by Black Flag, followed by the Go-Go's. In terms of cleanup, the punks were the worst. On punk nights, we'd get four hundred kids, all drunk and moshing. There'd be blood, sweat, and vomit all over the place; the floors would be sticky with spilled alcohol; and those wooden walls were porous. They absorbed all the smells. It was so nasty, and half the time David would be chasing Lizzie or me around. (He didn't dare hit on Dane.) We'd tell him, straight up, to fuck off. But he'd laugh, and before we knew it, he'd be hitting on us again. Dane used to razz me and Lizzie: "How about taking one for the team?"

The unwanted attention was worth it because David got us more gigs, and the more gigs we got, the more of a draw we became. Normally, if a band played the Starwood, it wouldn't get booked at the Whisky or the Troubadour for a couple of weeks. The clubs were jealous of each other's bands. But if you had enough juice, you could go back and forth, and you could ask for more money. I got good at that and at leveraging the bookers against one another. I'd go to the Whisky's booker and say, "Look, the Troubadour's giving us five hundred bucks for two nights, and the room can't even hold us. How about giving us seven hundred dollars for three nights?"

I didn't know if we could sell out three nights. But then we'd discover we could. Easily. We were now a big draw. And, at the same time, we were janitors. We'd pack the place at night and clean up after our own audience in the morning.

Even though Lizzie couldn't have built a chair or a table, he did know how to wire things. His dad was an electrician, and when Dane and I hammered together a few go-go boxes and put aluminum all along the sides, Lizzie figured out how we could make all these hundred-watt lights flicker on and off or chase one another.

The boxes were huge. No one else in town had them. I can still see Lizzie wiring them, with his hair swinging next to the drill.

A very old guy named Louie worked at the Starwood. He looked like a little gremlin who'd been there for one hundred years, and he was angry, always, at everyone. Louie took a liking to us. He had our best interests at heart in his own angry way. He passed by just as Lizzie was wiring and started yelling, "Hey, dumbass! You're going to wrap that drill around your head."

Lizzie looked up and said, "Hey, fuck you, Louie!"

Just as the words left his mouth, the drill caught Lizzie's hair and slammed into his head. Louie had to spend the next twenty minutes getting Lizzie untangled.

Those light boxes were one more thing to cart around. Lizzie had two Marshall stacks. Dane had his massive drum kit, and I had my own massive amps. John St. John's Hammond B3 weighed more than four hundred pounds, he had his huge Leslie cabinet, and on top of that, we had a PA and a keyboard riser. We didn't have

FRI & SAT, JUNE 20-21

NIGEL BENJAMIN

LIZZY GREY

DANE RAGE

LONDON

NIKKI SIXX

JOHN St. JOHN

STARWOOD
INFO 656-2200

roadies. We didn't have a van. We improvised everything. But we kept getting better. We worked on our stage moves, our makeup, our clothes. I started wearing an outfit that was half black, half black-and-white stripes. (Later on, in Mötley Crüe, I wore all black-and-white stripes.) In those days, a good cover band could make as much as $2,000 a night. Guys in LA were making anywhere between $4,000 and $8,000 a week, just playing covers. We played a few covers too. We'd start out shows with a Slade song, "Mama Weer All Crazee Now." (Quiet Riot covered that song on their big *Metal Health* album.) But we didn't play the Top 40, and more and more, we were playing originals: A song called "1980s Girl" in 1979—that's how clever we thought we were. A song called "Radio Stars." Lizzie and I had written "Public Enemy #1," a song that was on Mötley's first album. At the time, it wasn't as lucrative as playing sets full of covers. But it was the smart thing to be doing long-term. By the time we had become weekend headliners at the Starwood, we were already making anywhere from $1,000 to $2,000 a night. Even with a five-way split, we were bringing in money.

We kept plowing it into the band. We were still scrounging off women for our meals.

The Starwood had a rock room, where all the rock and punk bands used to play. The stairs leading up from that room led to a VIP area with a bar overlooking the stage. The stairs led down to another room full of old-school video games: Defender, Space Invaders, Asteroids. That was where Randy Rhoads and I hung out together before his departure for England. It led out to a big dance floor: the Starwood's disco room. The women who hung out in the disco room tended to be prettier than the women in the rock room. As a result, that's the side of the Starwood that Lizzie, Dane, and I gravitated toward. I'd lean against the wall. Women would come up to *us* now that London had become a known quantity.

The parking lot of the Rainbow was the spot too, after two in the morning. The Roxy was right next door—the clubs let out at the same time, and an ocean of kids would stream out. That parking lot was party central. It was hookup central. It's where you'd hear about underground shows or find girls to go home with. One night a girl came right up to us there and said, "Hey, want to come to a party? London's going to be there!"

"They are?"

"That's the rumor."

"You sure?"

We went. She'd used us to convince us, and because she had, she was right: there we were.

———

The Orchids were the girl band Kim Fowley formed after his old girl band, the Runaways, broke up. The last bass player to pass through the Runaways, Laurie McAllister, had gone on to play in the Orchids. But I had my eye on Laurie Bell, who played drums and sang in the band.

I met her backstage after one of their shows. I was with Lizzie and walked up to her, and she said, "What do you do?"

I was wearing my usual: tight pants; a black leather jacket; a cropped, ripped-up shirt; and high heels.

"I'm a dentist," I said, and we took it from there.

Laurie had moved to Los Angeles because Fowley had "discovered" Tom Johnson, the guy who was dating her sister. That was Fowley's thing. He was an impresario. He put musicians together and guided their careers. The younger the better, because that way he had control. Fowley turned Tom Johnson into Tommy Rock, and Tommy Rock had a couple of singles. Tom Johnson called Laurie up and said, "Come to LA. I told Fowley you could sing and play drums."

Laurie sang on a bunch of Fowley's demo recordings—songs he'd send out for artists to cover.

Fowley asked me to write one too, for Blondie. Back when I was still living with Angie, I wrote a riff and a couple of lines: "Stick to your guns / What's right for you ain't right for everyone." I hadn't gotten much further. But I fleshed the rest out and went down to Kim's weird apartment in Hollywood. It was rundown—a real shithole, with trash and pill bottles on every available surface. I thought, "This is it? The king of the strip lives in this dump?"

It was like meeting the wizard of Oz. Things were not as they appeared to us innocents. Then again, it *was* Hollywood.

Fowley liked the song. He gave me a hundred bucks and a deal that gave him 50 percent of the publishing. The next time I saw him, he told me Blondie had passed. I don't know to this day whether Debbie Harry even heard the song I had written. I kept it, and Mötley Crüe used it—it was the first song we recorded for our "Stick to Your Guns" / "Toast of the Town" seven-inch—and Fowley got a strong return on his investment.

Fowley had his name on "Cherry Bomb" too, and 50 percent of Joan Jett's money on another song that he'd never come near. And still he lived in that shithole apartment. I thought about him years later, on Mötley Crüe's Girls, Girls, Girls Tour. We'd given Guns N' Roses the opening slot, and Axl Rose told me, "You know, we worked 'Stick to Your Guns' up for *Appetite for Destruction*."

If they had used it, Fowley would have gotten his 50 percent all over again.

I was wary of him anyway. He'd walk up and down the Sunset Strip, juggling an apple and an orange with a crazed look in his eyes. But being crazy didn't make Fowley any less of a prick. I didn't like the guy, but I liked Laurie. I spent a lot of time at the Orchids' band house in Encino. Laurie was the businessperson in her band. I was the businessperson in mine. We planned. We strategized. Sometimes we played shows together. We'd walk down Hollywood Boulevard with a staple gun—I'd have Laurie up on my shoulders—and we'd go from one telephone pole to the next, putting up posters.

But I wasn't about to sit still for any one girl. I was twenty, and as far as I was concerned, I had just formed the next Rolling Stones.

I had turned twenty-one by the time I convinced Uncle Don to come down to the club. We were headlining now, two sets a night on Friday and Saturdays or on Saturdays and Sundays. We still had Nigel. We had John St. John. That was the best version of London there would ever be. Slash and Steve Adler rode their skateboards past the Starwood in those days. They'd sneak in through the back door and watch us. On the Girls, Girls, Girls Tour, they told me, "We'd see you onstage, we'd see Nigel, and we'd go, 'That's a rock band. That's a rock star. That's what we're going to be.'"

Inside the band, there were tensions. I was pushing for us to be faster and harder. I had already written most of the songs that were on Mötley Crüe's first album. But Nigel kept trying to bring in more syrupy songs.

I firmly believed that a rock record shouldn't have more than one ballad. By the same token, I didn't want to have more than one ballad per set. But ballads were Nigel's bread and butter. At one point, David Forrest and Gary Fontenot brought a deal to the table: we'd record in Japan and then go on tour in Europe. By the time we got back to the States, the record would be in distribution. It was never locked down—it was just an idea—but to us, it felt like our fantasy had come to pass.

Nigel wouldn't hear of it. He wouldn't sign the contract. He would not even look at the contract, he said, because they would want to promote us as hard rock.

I protested.

"But, Nigel, that's what we are! We're power pop crossed with glitter and hard rock!"

I recall his reply word for word: "If we're an apple, we don't want to be sold as a plum."

We should have been able to work it out. Nigel was stubborn, but so were we all. The problem, however, was that Nigel could be lazy too. He wouldn't write lyrics. Half the time he couldn't even be bothered to talk to the audience in ways that made sense.

"Nigel," I'd say. "You have to get them excited. You have to coax them into the tent."

"Bollocks. It don't fuckin' matter what I say. I could say, 'bowel cancer.' They'd fuckin' applaud."

Actually, with that accent, Nigel was right, and he knew it. He proved it to us that weekend. "The word for tonight is 'bowel cancer,'" he said from the stage, and the audience erupted. I've seen the same thing with other English bands: they'll get on stage, they'll say "carrots and peas!" and the audience goes wild. The accent goes a long way.

But on the night Uncle Don came to see us, the cracks in our firmament didn't show. That night we played like the brothers we had become.

I had waited until the last minute to tell the other guys. Christmas was around the corner, and we were driving on the Hollywood Freeway. At that time of year, the Capitol Records building always had a huge Christmas tree up on top, and I pointed at the tree and said, "Merry Christmas! That's our new record company."

"What are you talking about?"

"My uncle is finally coming to check us out."

When I had first mentioned Don, there had been a vague sense that, somewhere on down the line, I could get us an audition. Since then, enough time had passed that the other guys had the idea that if that were going to happen, it would have happened by now.

But Uncle Don came. He was wearing a sharp tailored suit. The A&R man who'd come with him was wearing a suit. No one else at the Starwood was wearing a suit. Everyone else at the Starwood was screaming because London had never been better. After the show, we were all drenched in sweat. We were walking on air. The adrenaline rush was fantastic, and when Don came backstage, we were grinning from ear to ear, beaming—every last one of us, including Nigel.

My uncle was very cordial. He was complimentary. He pulled me aside. "It's incredible," he said, "how far you've come in two years."

"Did you hear the audience? Did you hear them screaming for us?"

Uncle Don nodded. He smiled. He said, "Let's talk tomorrow."

I was so happy. Well past midnight, I called Nona and Tom, waking them up. I told them about Uncle Don.

I said, "I'm going to make it!"

I couldn't wait for the morning. I lay awake, thinking. Planning. As soon as I woke up, I picked up the phone.

"Frankie," Don said, "I think you've got a bright future. I think you have presence on stage. But, you know, it's not for us. I can't do it."

It was his right. He could just as easily have told me, "Frankie, it's not show family. It's show *business*."

I wasn't angry. I loved and respected my uncle. What I was, was confused and dejected. It was the last thing I had expected, a punch to the gut. I didn't know how to tell the other guys. Thinking about it made my stomach hurt.

I walked the length of the strip, back and forth, trying to imagine the best way to do it.

Fundamentally, nothing had changed. We had fought long and hard, scrapped our way to the top of the heap. We had the right singer. We had the right songs. We'd have to wait a bit longer, but there was no doubt we were going to make it.

By the time six o'clock rolled around, I had convinced myself that everything was okay. I bounced into rehearsal. I sat the guys down.

"Okay," I said. "I have good news and bad news."

"Let's have the good news!" said Lizzie.

"Start with the bad news," said Nigel.

"The bad news is, Capitol passed."

"Okay," said Nigel. "In that case, I'm quitting the band."

New Monster
Chapter 20

We walked around licking our wounds for a while. At that age, everything felt so immediate. To us, losing Nigel felt like the end of the world. But something inside me told me that I didn't have time to mope. Twenty-one didn't seem young at the time; it seemed old. I could hear the clock ticking.

Nigel's loss was a big setback, but we weren't back to square one. We had our audience. We had the songs. The last show we played was the best show we'd ever played. Afterward, we were the talk of the town. How hard could it be for the top band on the strip to find a new singer?

"Fuck Nigel Benjamin," I told the guys. "We're going to get Brian Connolly!"

Brian Connolly was the voice behind "Ballroom Blitz" and "Solid Gold Brass." He'd left Sweet by that point and recorded one single, but a solo album had not materialized.

I called Uncle Don and asked him, "Can you help me get ahold of Brian Connolly from Sweet?"

"Sure," Uncle Don said. "I'll give you an address."

I put together a package: a four-song demo we had recorded with Nigel, photos of us on stage, a typescript of our lyrics. It was as professional as I could make it. I spent a long time on the cover letter.

"Thank you for looking at our music," it read. "We're from Los Angeles. Nigel Benjamin was our singer. He didn't want to carry on, but you're our dream singer. We're called London, and you've been a big influence on our sound. What can we do to convince you to join us?"

I can only imagine what it would have been like for Brian to get a letter like that. "Okay, that's endearing. But we're really on different pages."

But I had been crushed by Uncle Don. I had been crushed by Nigel's leaving. I was desperate to get the okay, after mailing the package, to go ahead with a follow-up call.

I wasn't naive enough to think that Brian Connolly would drop everything, move to Los Angeles, and join my band. But at the least, I thought he'd have good advice. I could have used the encouragement. And I was just cocky enough to think, "Who knows? Anything's possible."

A year earlier, the thought of Nigel Benjamin in London would have seemed just as ridiculous.

Finally, the call from Don came. On a Friday. I was lucky he got me at home. Because of the time difference, Don said that I was to call Connolly on Saturday at eight in the morning.

I called at that time, precisely, and heard two quick rings in a row. That was the sound of a UK landline. I'd only heard it in the movies. I could hear my heart beating as well, until Connolly picked up the phone.

"'Ello."

"Hi. It's Nikki Sixx. I'm Don Zimmerman's nephew."

"Oh. Great, right. Listen. Thank you. Looks lovely. But I'll have to pass."

"Did you hear our demo?" I sputtered. "Our songs, they're all hits. Did you see the photos? The band? This is what's needed right now. The right look. The right sound."

"I'm sorry," Connolly said. "I like your uncle. I'm sure you're a very nice kid—"

I bit my lip.

"—but rock and roll's over. It's dead and gone now. It's not coming back. I'm making my country album."

We had a fan named Carole McSweeney who worked as a law clerk at Mitchell Silberberg & Knupp, one of the big entertainment firms in Los Angeles. Carole had seen us several times at the Starwood, and she and I had developed a platonic friendship. We'd go down to the Hamburger Hamlet on Sunset, and we'd strategize. Carole would talk about her dreams. She was in law school; she wanted to write.

I would tell her about mine.

It wasn't just Uncle Don. Rock and roll really was struggling. To get signed in 1980, you needed to have a short haircut and a skinny tie. You needed to be the Knack, not Deep Purple. A mod, not a rocker. But I was rocked out to the fullest degree. All I could think about in those days was, "What can I do to make my band *more* outrageous?" We tied bones in our hair. We overdid our makeup. We weren't the Plimsouls. We weren't punk rock. We loved the

Ramones and the Pistols, but we loved Cheap Trick and Aerosmith too. Punk was all about subtraction: How much could you take away to get down to the essence? The Ramones had done that. They stripped out the solos, sped everything up. I admired their intensity and attitude. But when it came to my own songs, I didn't want less—I wanted more. I wanted *more* solos. I wanted vocals that did more than bark. I wanted to be in a band that could soar, dive-bomb, and soar—all in the same song.

I wasn't a minimalist. I was drawn to excess. My whole life was extreme and excessive. Drugs weren't a problem. We didn't know about AIDS. Life revolved around music and fighting and drinking and fucking. When I was in London, those were my cardinal points. There were no grown-ups around, no rules. I was desperate, but I wasn't uptight. I wasn't East Coast neurotic. Why in the world would I have wanted to sound like the Knack?

That's what I'd talk about with Carole, who believed in me. She loved my band. I didn't have to impress her. I thought of her as a sister, and I wasn't trying to get her in bed. With her, it was easier to open up.

I told Carole things I never would have talked about with Lizzie or Dane. I didn't have a safety net. I didn't have any money. I had dropped out of school in tenth grade, I had no mom and no dad, and the only real home I had to go home to was in Idaho. I'd talk about that too. The incredible frustration of being able to make a room full of kids lose their minds—set after set, night after night—and yet we couldn't get signed.

It was like living inside a bubble. That's why I got into so many fights. On punk night at the Starwood, I'd egg the punks on. I didn't care if I got my ass kicked as long as I got my licks in. I would come home bruised and bloodied, but I needed the fire. I needed the heat. Something wasn't connecting, and I had a need to connect.

I needed to shatter the bubble.

We got a new singer named Michael White, but we knew he wasn't going to be a good fit. We'd gone down the same road with Henry Valentine. Michael White sounded and looked too much like Robert Plant—so much so that he was the singer in a Led Zeppelin cover band. The chemistry wasn't there. But Michael had the best voice out of anyone we had auditioned, and London needed to play. We had finally climbed to the top of the Sunset Strip mountain—we were right where Quiet Riot had been when London was just starting out—and we had to maintain our position, our following, our name.

We felt like we had built this monster, and the monster was telling us, "Feed me."

I felt better after we rehearsed and rehearsed. I had to admit, we didn't sound bad. Not the way we'd sounded with Nigel, but Nigel's absence left more room for me to push for what I'd always pushed for: harder, faster, heavier, *more.*

I never got to the point where I was thrilled about this new incarnation of London. To me, it felt like we were still treading water. But I also had to admit, it beat drowning.

It had been a few weeks since we had seen David Forrest. Gary was out of it too half the time. Things had become druggy up on the management level. They always had been, but now they were starting to spin off the rails. We saw shady things out of the corners of our eyes: guns and samurai swords, bricks of cocaine and heroin, giant jars full of quaaludes, glass pipes. We didn't want to know, but we heard stories. I was drawn to violence, darkness, and death as subjects for my songs. But this was different. This was the place where we worked, where we played, where we lived. Nash had all these goons working for him, bodyguards who were the size of professional wrestlers. They were around more and more, and even though we were employed by the club, they didn't go out of their way to be friendly. If we were doing something in their way, they wouldn't say, "Excuse me." They'd shoulder us aside, like you would a curtain made out of glass beads.

When we first started, we ran rum and Cokes back to David's office. Todd Rundgren would be hanging out. John Holmes, the porn star, would be there. We'd stick around, starstruck, and hear a few stories about the glory days. But we hadn't seen Rundgren around in a year, and every time we saw John Holmes, he looked that much worse for wear—more emaciated, glassy-eyed, almost feral. Our sound guy, Dom Fragomel, was starting to look like that too. So was Gary, when Lizzie and I went to see him to ask about David and booking some shows. Some of the stuff that came out of his mouth made no sense. He was so high he was talking in circles. But someone had to be booking the club.

We got him to write a phone number down. I called. David answered.

"Nikki!" he said, talking a mile a minute. "That's great! That's terrific! Of course you can play! Do you want a Friday or Saturday?"

I told him. We played. We sounded like London fronted by a poor man's Robert Plant. But we didn't sound terrible. We got a response. The audience called us back for an encore. The real problem came at the end of the night, when we went down to the office to get paid.

The door was locked. There was nobody there.

There was no one there on Monday either. When I called David's number, he didn't pick up.

We had filled the room. We were owed $2,000. Michael went off on us, threatened to quit, and he was within his rights. We didn't know what to tell him. We tried and tried. But we couldn't get paid. We had shows coming up the following weekend. How were we going to play them—and convince Michael to sing—when we hadn't been paid for the last one?

We didn't know Eddie Nash. We had seen him in the clubs: an olive-skinned guy, Middle Eastern, coked out. But we had never really spoken to him. Now, we decided, we'd have to.

David Forrest had given me a silver Vega—a terrible car with a lawnmower engine that was always being recalled because the engines overheated, cracked, or caught fire. We drove it down to Ali Baba's, but the manager told us he hadn't seen Eddie for weeks. We went down to the Kit Kat Club, and the manager there said the same thing. We tried the Soul'd Out and the Paradise. We drove all over Hollywood before ending up at Nash's tiki bar, the Seven Seas.

We told the hostess who we were and who we worked for. She told us that we were lucky. She hadn't seen Nash for weeks either, but he was here now, in the back.

We walked through the kitchen. The cooks were carving up big hunks of meat with their cleavers. At the bottom of a set of stairs, we saw one of Nash's big goons. He was wearing a suit, and the bulge his gun made was visible—that was the point.

We were wearing leather pants—Lizzie was wearing his tube top—and we were in heels. But the bodyguard was as tall as we were.

Dane spoke first. "We're here to see Eddie Nash."

"What about?"

"He owes us money."

The goon frowned. Then he started to chuckle. "Okay," he said. "Follow me."

The four of us went upstairs to an office that was small, poorly lit, dingy. It could have just as easily been owned by some seedy accountant, except for one more bodyguard who was there.

Eddie was there too, glassy-eyed in a leather chair behind the desk. With six of us there, it was crowded in that tiny office.

"What's the deal, guys?" Nash asked.

This time, Lizzie spoke up. "We played a show at the Starwood. We never got paid."

"So?"

"So we came here to get paid," I said.

Eddie looked us up and down. He looked at his goons. Then he started laughing, and both of his bodyguards started to laugh.

"I don't think I owe you anything," he said. "What do you think about that?"

The three of us looked at each other. We thought of the stories we'd heard. Stories about broken bones. The kinds of beatdowns you didn't come back from.

The whole week had turned into a kick in the balls.

"Yeah," we said. "Yeah, we're all good. We're okay."

We weren't okay. The first thing Michael asked that night at rehearsal was, "Where's my money?"

I didn't know what to tell him. "Give me two hours," I said.

I got into my Vega and started to drive.

I couldn't call Uncle Don. He'd turned my band down, and I had my pride.

I couldn't call Nona and Tom. For months I'd been telling them, truthfully, about how successful my band was.

I couldn't call my mom because I didn't know where she was.

Then I had the idea: "Fuck it. My old man never lifted a finger to help me. It's four hundred bucks. The least he can do now is cough up some money."

I can still sort of see what I was thinking. For years I had been furious at my dad, but I would let go of all that for what was really a very small price. I would let bygones be bygones, and I would be doing it just like that, then and there.

As far as I was concerned, my father was getting off cheap.

I wasn't thinking, "I'm a bit lost, and I feel so alone." But at a deeper level, I must have been feeling it. This was the closest I could come at the time to admitting I needed my father, his love, the connection.

I pulled up next to a payphone. I called 411 and gave the operator the name my father had given me: "Frank Feranna."

I dialed the number. A woman picked up.

"Hello?"

"Hi," I said. "This is Frank."

"What? Who is this?"

"Frank Feranna."

I held my breath through the long pause that followed.

"Frank Feranna is dead. He died two years ago."

I was stunned. I wanted to sit on the sidewalk. I wanted to throw things. I wanted to throw up. I started to cry.

"This is his son, Frankie," I said.

"I don't know why you'd be calling," the woman said. "Don't call again."

I got back in my Vega and drove. I don't know if it was raining. I don't recall parking outside the Spotlight. I only remember

FRANCES SALVATO
JOSEPH FELICE
IDA MAY SCHLAUDT

RUTH SELSLEAD
PAULINE SESSAREGO
FRANK FERANNA

DOROTHY SMOKER
MABLE SNODGRASS

going upstairs where the guys were in the hall with Michael, waiting for me.

"You have to give me a few more days."

"No," Michael told me. "I don't. I don't have to do anything. Fuck you. I quit."

I could feel myself sliding down the mountain, but I had my claws dug deep down in the soil. I didn't want to hit bottom. I couldn't, because all that was waiting for me at the bottom was a Greyhound and a bus ticket back to Idaho.

"Nikki," said Lizzie, "it's going to be okay. We'll get a new singer."

We were in my Vega, idling outside of the Starwood.

"Lizzie," I said. "It's not working. I can't count on it working. The only thing I can count on is me."

Lizzie started to cry. "Well, you can't be in a band by yourself."

I would have cried too, but I was cried out. Lizzie had always felt like my brother, but now I felt nothing, and I stood my ground. "I know that. But I have to do things my way."

The next day, I called Carole. When we met at Hamburger Hamlet, I told her about my dad and my band.

I told her, "Frank Feranna is dead. I want to make it official."

Carole got what I was saying.

"It's going to be okay," she said. "I'll help you."

I didn't know whether to cry or to laugh.

"I wish everyone would quit telling me things are going to be okay."

True to her word, Carole helped me. Later that week, we went down to the courthouse.

Carole had told me, "Dress as conservatively as you can."

I interpreted that to mean, "Wear motorcycle boots, not the stilettos." But I couldn't have dressed conservatively if I'd wanted to. I didn't have any conservative clothes. Plus, I had been on a bit of a bender: a bottle of vodka a night. Carole picked me up at wherever it was I was staying. At 7:15 a.m., she had to pound on the door before waking me up. I had makeup on that was all smeared. I had on a cropped, sleeveless T-shirt and tight-fitting black pants. My head was throbbing. But we got to the courthouse on time. We took a seat on the bench. We waited for what seemed like a very long time until my name was called.

"Franklin Feranna!"

Carole poked me awake.

I jumped up, and the judge gave a withering look. He was an old guy, square and grumpy.

"Sit down," he said. "You want to change your name?"

"I'm a performer," I told him. "I want to use my stage name."

"So, use it. Who's stopping you? What kind of name is Nikki Sixx, anyway?"

"It's my name. It's the name I want to use for the rest of my life."

"And your parents approve of this?"

"I'm twenty-one. Don't need parents."

"Have you thought about how this will make them feel? Have you thought about your grandparents?"

The judge would not let it go. "Has your mother approved? Has your father approved?"

"My father's dead," I told him.

With each question, I'd slouched farther and farther down on the bench. By now, I was sitting on the floor, practically, looking down at the scuffs on my boots.

The judge looked down too. He shuffled some papers. "Okay," he said. "Have it your way."

Carole went up to the clerk. Court was breaking for lunch by that point, so she said, "Can you mail out the order?"

FRANKLIN CARLTON FERANNA
2012 Lemoyne Street
Los Angeles, California   90026
(213) 662-9047
IN PROPRIA PERSONA

ORIGINAL FILED

OCT - 3 1980

CE: ...CT
COUNTY CLERK

SUPERIOR COURT OF THE STATE OF CALIFORNIA

FOR THE COUNTY OF LOS ANGELES

C340460

IN RE THE MATTER OF THE APPLICATION)   CASE NO.
OF FRANK CARLTON FERANNA,   )
)   PETITION FOR CHANGE OF
)   NAME
FOR CHANGE OF NAME.   )
)

      IN CONNECTION with his application for change of name,
Petitioner, FRANKLIN CARLTON FERANNA, sets forth the following
information concerning himself, as required by Section 1276 of the
Code of Civil Procedure:

      1.   Born on December 11, 1958, in San Jose, California.

      2.   Residence: 11298 Maranda Street, North Hollywood,
California.

      3.   Present name: FRANKLIN CARLTON FERANNA.

      4.   Proposed name: NIKKI SIXX.

      5.   Reason for change: Petitioner is a performing Artist
and will utilize the new name in the course and scope of his
profession in the entertainment business.

/ / / / /

/ / / / /

"I can," the clerk said. "But it will take a long time to arrive. Would you like to write it out by hand?"

Carole said, "Sure." And she did. Nikki Sixx was the guy who walked out of that courthouse, blinking in the cold, hot light of the day.

The sun was beating down, my head was pounding, and my mouth was dry.

"So, Nikki," Carole said, "what are you going to do now?"

"I'm going to build a new monster," I said.

Stick to Your Guns

Chapter 21

When I was little, I didn't know what the feeling was called. A combination of awe, curiosity, and adventure. In Lake Tahoe I was always out and exploring. I'd dig a hole under some fallen tree. Cover it with an old tarp. Cover that with branches, leaves, and anything else I could find (even dirt) to secure the secret location. Then the real fun would begin: I'd sit in my new foxhole—and if I had a friend there, then so much the better. We daydreamed. We lost ourselves. And at dusk we raced off on banana bikes that we imagined to be Harley-Davidson motorcycles.

I guess that I've been daydreaming for as long as I can remember. For just as long, I've been writing those daydreams down on scraps of paper. Dozens, then hundreds, then thousands of them.

Writing songs is the same thing. A form of exploring. Of losing myself. Creativity, coming up with new ideas, and collaboration: for me, those are the most thrilling things.

As a kid, I would hum my own melodies over songs I heard on the radio (and, later on, vinyl records). As I got older, I played along on my bass or guitar. But I was never great at learning other people's songs. Halfway through, I would be writing my own.

I didn't name it at the time. I didn't think of it as songwriting. It was more like wanderlust. And, for sure, there have been obstacles along the way. There may not be a road map, but there are definitely roadblocks to creativity. There's a critic that lives in all of our heads. My mission is not to slow down or—worse—let that critic stop me from creating.

That's what stream of consciousness is. Think all you want, but don't think while you're making.

Thinking and making are opposite things.

We're all different. And we're all prisoners in our own heads. But one thing that fascinates me is the way every person has their own way to get ideas *out* of their heads. That's where collaboration can be very helpful—having a friend in your foxhole. It's hard to know when inspiration will strike. It's hard to know what will spark it. But collaboration can double your chances.

Here are a few other tricks I've used whenever there's too much mud built up on my tires:

* What other people might make of what you are creating is none of your business. Chasing trends or even following them is a deadly poison—not just to the process but to the outcome.
* Keith Richards walks around with a guitar. He's always playing, and I find that admirable. But it's not what I do. I spend a lot of time waiting. But I stay in shape, practicing, reading, and writing. I try to stay limber. I've learned over the years that when ideas do come, they come down all at once, in an avalanche. You'd better be ready.
* Once the lyric, the poem, or the idea for a song appears, I need a quiet place I like to go to and be in. I'll always sit down on the ground. Something about sitting cross-legged, bent all the way over one of my notebooks, helps me to connect.

    I guess you could say that it's grounding.

Most of the time I have a circle of books—random books—all around me. People have said that it looks like I'm conjuring. Maybe I am. Whatever it is, it seems to work.

* A lot of my songs don't rhyme. Not exactly. I just let it flow out. I've been known to write four full pages of lyrics without stopping to come up for air.

* If I do hit a wall, I reach for the nearest book in my circle, open it to a random page, and point to a random sentence. The rule is, I have to use one of the words in that sentence.

It's not an ironclad rule. You can always cut the word later. You can cut the entire couplet. Cutting is as important as building up. Once the word serves its purpose, it's fine to discard. The important thing is to keep moving.

Try it yourself. What I find is that it stops me from thinking about the hurdle in front of me. It puts me back in the race. My heart starts to pound. It feel like I am about to uncover some secret—some treasure—and truthfully, sometimes I do. We can talk about minor and major chords, key signatures, and key changes all day, but then we'd be thinking, not doing.

* Stay loose. Stay open. Keep a notepad nearby. If inspiration strikes, be ready to pull over to the side of the road. At the same time, protect your creative space. Keep the noise out. Keep out the gatekeepers, naysayers, negators, and inhibitors. Dismantle, dispose of them, ASAP. Surround yourself with creative things: books, paintings, photographs, records. Surround yourself with creative people.

* Dream big. Be fearless. Learn to practice long-term thinking, not short-term thinking, in your life and in your work. The worst that can happen is that you'll fail. And the best that will happen is that you *will* fail, because failing—sometimes even in front of a crowd—is what lights a real fire under your ass. If we all knew ahead of time that *these* things and not *those* things would work, then we'd all be billionaires. But since

we're all stumbling around in the dark, the least we can do is get comfortable with trial and error.

* It doesn't take ten thousand hours to master your craft. It takes a lifetime, and that's the best thing. A lifetime is what you happen to have.

* Believe in yourself, even when no one else does. Believe in yourself *especially* when no one else does. Don't be afraid to walk away from mistakes. But if you know in your heart of hearts that you're right, then stick with it. Every bold new idea was seen, at some point, as a threat. But if you're right and you stick to your guns, the world will come around. That's what "Stick to Your Guns," that song I wrote for Blondie, is about: "You got to stick to your guns / What's right for you ain't right for everyone."

* Don't underestimate the role that luck plays. Successful people tend to do that: chalk their achievements up to their intelligence, diligence, good looks, or charm. The truth is, at some point, they probably got lucky—and that's nothing to be ashamed of. Luck comes and goes. The trick is to stay in great shape so that when it does come, you can seize it. The really big break might not come your way twice. So when it does come, don't waste it.

* If there was a road map, it would look a lot like that. My map, at least. The path of creativity. And for me, staying spiritually connected to something greater than myself is also crucial. Arrogance is the opposite of making too. I try to celebrate life and stay humble.

The story I've told in these pages ends on December 9, 1980. That's the day I legally changed my name to Nikki Sixx. Two days later,

I turned twenty-two. A few weeks later, on January 17, Mötley Crüe officially formed. A few months after that, on April 24, 1981—a Friday—Mötley Crüe played its first show. The location? The Starwood, of course.

Things went south for the club after that. Eddie Nash and John Holmes got tangled up in the Wonderland killings—also known as the "Four on the Floor" murders, although I have heard there was just as much blood on the walls and the ceilings. If you've seen *Boogie Nights* or the film *Wonderland*, with Val Kilmer, you already know it's one hell of a story. If not, go ahead—take the time to Google it. You'll see how lucky we were backing away from Ed Nash and his goons that one day.

Mötley Crüe was a monster right out of the gate. Before long, we were headlining up and down the Sunset Strip. We were the best, biggest band in the clubs, and once again I got Uncle Don to come down and see us play.

Once again, Uncle Don passed on my band.

Years later, after we had sold tens of millions of records and headlined all over the world, Don told me, "Failing to sign Mötley Crüe was the biggest professional mistake that I made." But all that it did at the time was inspire me to double down. We cut our first album that year, and taking a page out of the punk rock playbook, we formed our own label—Leathür Records—to distribute it.

The rest is history. For forty years, I've kept Mötley Crüe together, weathering storms in the industry, storms in our lives. With Allen Kovac, I overrode my own lawyer's advice, stuck to my guns, and wrestled control of our masters away from Elektra, the label that we had eventually signed to. Unlike the vast majority of rock bands, we own the music we've made, going all the way back to day one.

When it was time to write my own book, I came up with *The Heroin Diaries*. Not the easiest sell for a first-time author. Not the sexiest subject. But an important one. So I stuck to my guns and wrote the book, and when I was done, I sat down with DJ Asha and James Michael and wrote "Life Is Beautiful"—a song that summed up sobriety. Darkness is narrow, but recovery is broad. That's what helped turn *The Heroin Diaries* into a best-selling book.

Then I went on the road and read to thousands of people. I stayed late at every book signing, made sure to shake every hand, hear every story. It took hours and hours, but every one of those hours was worth it. Then James, DJ, and I forged ahead with Sixx A.M., making five studio albums and writing songs that explore real-life themes, feelings, and subjects that other rock bands might not touch.

At the same time, Allen had an idea: "You like Wolfman Jack," he told me. "You love Alan Freed. You love Jim Ladd. Why not do that? You've got the voice. You love to tell stories. What those guys did for you, you could do for a new generation of rock bands."

Once again Allen was right: I loved to get on the air and tell stories. I've never stopped being a fan. I love to play rock music in front of an audience, and this was another way for me to do that. A way for me to find new bands and up-and-comers and help them along too. I had a new captive audience. Why wouldn't I want to expose them to exciting new music? I'm a big believer in paying it forward. In passing it on.

So that's what I did—and for eight years straight, my show, *Sixx Sense*, was the top-rated syndicated radio show in the country.

Every one of those years was a blast.

Then, after sixteen years of turnarounds and an ever-revolving cast of producers and production heads, we finally managed to get our film done and usher it out into the world. That would never have happened if we'd been afraid of pissing off the gatekeepers. If we'd been cowed by the lawyers, studios, record companies, book publishers, and gallery heads. We never would have accomplished a thing.

Take the big chances. And stick to your guns. What's right for you ain't right for everyone.

I'm passionate about all of it. Passionate about art. Passionate about music. I'm straight-up obsessed with photography. I'm proud of my platinum albums, sure. But the thing I may be proudest of, outside of my kids, is having a Leica camera named after me. I've always had street smarts, but I've also been ready and willing to learn from those who know more. The key, for me, is to be more ambitious with each successive outing. Don't just write a book; write a soundtrack to a book. And make sure that the story you're telling resonates and helps people who may be going through some of the same stuff you've gone through. Think outside of the box. And think bigger each time you go out, no matter what the project might be. It's important to leave some sort of mark in this life. And it's just as important to pass the baton.

The trick for us all is to think big but stay humble, because we never know where new ideas will come from and because collaboration keeps our minds young and nimble. Speaking for myself, I know I can't hit it out of the park every day, but I'm always ready to get up to bat. And, honestly, my batting average ain't bad.

I look back now, here in Wyoming. Out on my rock, gazing out at the elk, I look back and think, "Whoa. What if that kid had not gotten on that Greyhound bus? Had not been fearless? Had not made some of the mistakes that he made? Had not taken chances?"

I don't know where I'd be today, but I wouldn't be here.

Tom told me once about an idea he'd had—an invention—that he'd never gotten around to patenting.

I said, "Why not?"

Tom hemmed and hawed a bit. He didn't have a good answer. But I can venture some guesses: He didn't have the education. He didn't have an Allen Kovac to advise him. But he still gave me so much. Watching Tom work, watching his determination and focus, seeing him take care of Nona and his family—this is where I got my own work ethic and never-say-die attitude. Sometimes, out on the road, I'd get tired. I'd seen Tom get tired too. But Tom never stopped moving, and neither did I—because stopping was never an option. At the end of the night, there's the show.

The guitar goes up high. The bass goes down low. It sounds like a row of jet engines.

It's the same sound I heard in my head in Twin Falls. In Jerome. The same, but maybe better. And whatever sound or idea you've got in your head, my advice is, lean into it. You never know where it'll take you.

NIKKI SIXX / FRANK FERANNA

Acknowledgments

I have my mom and my dad, Nona and Tom, Don and Sharon, and Bob and Harlene to thank for a lot of my first twenty-one. I want thank Allen Kovac for being my head coach and helping me manifest all my crazy ideas. Thanks to Chris Nilsson and Konstanze Louden for being my think-outside-the-box managers and to Crystal Torres, Rohan Ocean, and Will Mingrone at 10th Street Entertainment.

Thanks to Dennis Arfa and Pete Pappalardo at AGI for keeping my ass on the road.

At Better Noise Music, I'd like to thank Dan Lieblein, Steve Kline, Joe McFadden, Rose Slanic, Jackie Kajzer, Debra Stella, Dan Waite, Bryan Raisa, Tim Mclean Smith, Sean Maxson, Omar Rana, Bjorn Meyer, Victor Lang, Jimmy Harney, Amy O'Connor, Lexie Viklund, Daniel Sears, Eoin Wenger, Brittany Deeney, Ben Guzman, Sarah Waxberg, Henry Tongue, Autumn Myers, and Claudia Mancino.

Thanks to Doug Mark at Mark Music & Media Law, PC, and Pam Malek at Glass Malek LLP.

Thanks to Barry Drinkwater, Benny Lindstroem, Mike Rotondo, and Katy Ables at Global Merchandising, Ltd.

At Hachette, I'd like to thank my editor, Brant Rumble, who argued with me, down the line, and let me win one every once in a while. Thanks, Brant. While we're at it, I'd like to thank their whole team: Michelle Aielli, Michael Barrs, Caitlyn Budnick, Andreas Campomar, Michael Clark, Joelle Dieu, Sarah Falter, Amanda Kain (the art director who got this book's cover started before going out on maternity leave), Richard Ljoenes (who designed the actual cover), Molly Morrison, Mary Ann Naples, Monica Oluwek, Laura Piasio, Megan Schindele, Mollie Weisenfeld, and Sarah Wood, the art director who saw the cover through.

Thanks to Laura Ferreiro.

Thanks to Joe Lalich for working late into the night designing the interior and scrapbooks with me. Proper villain, for sure.

Thanks to Alex Abramovich for writing this book with me. Pushing me, listening to me, being willing to argue with me, never taking the clickbait route, and, most of all, having a never-dying vision to make this book honest in all accounts. It was an honor.

The book was a perfect occasion to revisit dear friends and family members. The pandemic might have kept us apart spatially, but I am eternally grateful for the time Bob and Harlene took over the phone. I'm equally grateful to Don and Sharon's daughter, Michele Amburgey, for her time and generosity. And, of course, I'm thankful for my sister Ceci for her willingness to walking back down memory lane.

This book gave me a good reason to connect with other folks, too. It was fantastic to catch up with Alan Weeks, Mike "Bubba" Garcia, and Susan Bond—I knew her as Susie Maddo—in and around Jerome. To reconnect with Rick and Linda Van Zandt, who are still together, up there in Seattle, and with Dane Scarborough (Dane Rage), who's in LA, still surfing, still playing drums, and working as an inventor and entrepreneur.

Thanks to John St. John for the laughs.

Thanks to Lizzie's wife, Jennifer; to their two daughters, Annabelle and Ariel; and to Lizzie's sister Susan Victoria Brandon.

Carole Garner McSweeney listened to my rock-and-roll dreams, was a good friend when I needed a friend, and helped me get my name changed. Thank you.

Thanks to Ramon Rodriquez, who gave me that first, old guitar.

Thanks to Angie Diehl, who was so generous with her memories, her photographs, and her scrapbooks.

Don Adkins took all those amazing photos of London. Thanks for capturing the times so well so that we could relive them so vividly.

Thanks to Ché Zuro.

Thanks to Laurie Bell for the inside info on those innocent times.

Katie Kastel dug deep to find that fantastic, previously unseen photo of fresh-faced seventeen-year-old me.

Thanks most of all to my five beautiful children.

And, of course, to my ride-or-die, my love, my wife: Courtney.

HITS is the ultimate SIXX: A.M. collection, featuring twenty tracks
including the new song and book-companion single "The First 21"

Also includes two additional unreleased tracks,"Penetrate" and "Waiting All My
Life," plus new mixes of "Talk to Me," "Skin," and the iconic
"Life Is Beautiful"

"The First 21" is a new song from Sixx: A.M., and it's a throwback
to the emotional times we all had growing up discovering music,
ourselves, and our dreams. It's a song about coming of age
and leans heavily on great songwriting from the 1970s.

Available on CD, Vinyl & Digital